strange things i've named

poetry & prose

by

julius henry

Once young, I thought the following poems and prose and, more importantly, theories would change not only me but the world around me. I was wrong. My works failed me. Therefore, the following works should be viewed as nothing more than the naïve attempts of a foolish waif to alter perception and reality.

ISBN: 978-0-6151-4282-1

Published in the United States of America

First published April 2007

strange things i've named

poetry & prose

by

julius henry

for Arthur Rimbaud
& Isidore Ducasse

Ten points of interest to the aspiring Verbatimist
(including arguments)

1. Be completely honest. Don't hold anything back. If a thought pops into your head write it out, even if it is completely against everything you believe in or stand for. Don't push any thought to the side.

Rebuttal: What if I don't want to explore the darkest regions of my mind?

Reply: Then you will never be a *Verbatimist.* Darkness is the most potent weapon in a *Verbatimist's* arsenal.

2. Shake people to the core. Make them confront their deepest fears. Make them embrace their dreams.

Rebuttal: Art should be a form of entertainment & escapism.

Reply: Then go to Hollywood. You'll be a great asset there.

3. Represent who you are as a person & an ideal through your works. Never create anything you can't wrap your head around. Don't leave chance to the pen. Writing about what you do not know can be detrimental to your survival as a writer.

Rebuttal: Well, how am I supposed to create intriguing plots & interesting characters if I can't make stuff up?

Reply: You don't have to 'make stuff up' in order to fascinate & intrigue people. The mysteries & enigmas of the human mind are infinitely more interesting than anything you could manufacture.

4. You are not an artist. You do not create art. You write, paint, etc. Leave the categories & classifications to those who only view it from afar.

Rebuttal: If I'm not an artist how can I be a *Verbatimist*?

Reply: *Verbatimism* & art are two different entities. In theory one could be a *Verbatimist* without ever writing, painting, etc.

5. Burn every book you own. Forget every book you've read. Don't consciously quote—or reference—anything.

Rebuttal: I don't mind wearing my influences on my sleeve. Why would I want to ignore those who inspired me to do this in the first place?

Reply: You're not ignoring anyone. Your subconscious mind records & remembers everything. What you *are* doing is making a conscious effort to not show off.

6. Change the shape of the world in the clouds. Rewrite history. Create everything as if it was born in your mind. Nothing is bad. Let's remove the scholarly notions of separating works. Everything is unified. Nothing is superior. Nothing is inferior. Everything is beautiful & holy.

Rebuttal: But what if it parallels a work by someone who came before me?

Reply: Then it does. The point is that nothing is done wrong or badly. If one so desires to ignore basic syntactical & grammatical rules then he will not be punished or frowned on for doing so.

7. Challenge the taboos & conventions of the day. Everything should remain suspicious until you've reinterpreted it. Allow nothing to suppress your creativity, no matter how vile & nauseating it may be.

Rebuttal: What if I don't want to disgust or offend people?

Reply: People are sensible beings. If they can't tolerate a strong or violent image than they will simply move on or abolish it. You are not here to censor yourself & care for others. Point number 7 is important to your growth as a *Verbatimist.*

8. Suppress nothing. Hide nothing. Speak of everything w/ total honesty.

Rebuttal: What if I'm hanging onto secrets I don't know how to accept or deal with?

Reply: Then you will never be a *Verbatimist.* You must confront & develop at least a *partial* understanding of every facet of your psyche. It is the only way. This is the one rule that *cannot* be broken.

9. Be truthful to yourself & everything will work out in the end

Rebuttal: What if I can't do it?

Reply: What if you can?

10. Be Great.

Rebuttal: What if I can't do it?

Reply: What if you can?

VENI, VIDI, VICI.

I.

A Deluge of Blood

1998-2000

The intent of art is to implant into our neurotic
shells the burning seeds of dementia—to transcend the
purity of divine words—of meaning—there is no meaning
in this decadent age—only definition—art should represent
schizophrenia—O' ghosts
inexhaustible deity
leave my head
my fuckin mind
alone
you goddamn rabid
dogs—for schizophrenia is the goal we must set
for ourselves—or we burn in this organic cauldron—that
rots—suspended—in space—insanity is the door that must be
unhinged—or senses atrophy—and salvation lies in a complete
unraveling of the senses—the doors of perception are loaded
with explosives—go ahead—blow it off its hinges—it's the
only way—you see—schizophrenia is labeled as an insidious
disease—it is neither disease nor anomaly but a step *up*
in evolution—it is immaculate in form—an opening of all the
senses—complete freedom—of thought—mannerisms—even
physiognomy—it is everything Dionysus represented—no longer
the artist he has himself become the work of art—it is
complete atrophy of reason—of objectivity—*subjectivity*—it
is the fourth dimension—total annihilation of the body and
mind—you choke

on the

juices of

your bleeding

tongue—

it is a million uninhibited souls dancing naked in the streets—it is teenage girls soaking your sheets with virgin blood—it transcends this doomed meat coil and becomes the quintessential being—once again souls are displayed on the *outside*—for art—in this late hour of the century—has become nothing more than mere *ornamentation*—a novelty—an esoteric language spoken by men of a seemingly higher class—it is *guided* rather than *guiding*—art should lay the foundation for civilization—not the other way around—

it has been injected with reason and meaning—or a shell thereof—with *intelligentsia*—yes my friends—that condescending hand that claims to hold the deed to reason—it is for these reasons—my dear sweet friends—that we must create a new form of art—represent the mind verbatim—strip ourselves

of these moral clothes—watch the mad dynamos separate into thousands of pieces and splinter the sunset

I am a man—I am a god—witness
the birth of a new form of literature—
witness the rotting corpses of our buried
pasts—the soaring fountains of meat and
blood—where words flow like water—the
cacklin jackals laugh at your satire—your
emptiness is open—brutal honesty grips you
like cancerous fists—and eyeballs
are cinematic windows—all words are mere
words but liquid words excite me—I hold
cancer like vodka—see—and uncontrolled
visions of bloody orgasms explode in
your head—don't hold back—
I rammed my fist hard—skin ripped—she
cried the brutal cry of dying cats—
shut up you bloody bitch—
insanity travels through high tension
wires—step right up girls and bitches and
witness the puzzlin prose of this here
proxy—bring yer turbans in a hat—don't
show yer pierced snatch—I wanna feel it in
the dark—her juices stained my forearm—I
swam on her back—I watched the moon—
don't hold back—
I fucked the immaculate moonlight while her

shadow bounced on my lap—my
children swam in the dead ozone—
click—flick—lick—roll those fingers off
yer bones—see—nothin to it—all that
rhetorical bullshit in the past is nothing
but linear insanity—bloody orgasms—skin
rip—she cried—shut up you bloody bitch—
her gardens fluttered—there is only
one—I am god—her canyons sighed
as the moonlight snatched the
fading remnants of her innocence—
you belong to me—I whisper in her ear—
I have saturated your blood with my
essence—I'll hurt you like junk—go ahead—
wash—you can't free yourself of me—I
won't stop till your oceans're dried up—
I'll eat every inch or your salty flesh
and perfectly shaved gardens—now I demand
you eat the fruit from my tree of knowledge—
I love her—sixteen year old whore—like
fuckin your daughter—
see—not bad—
could use some improvement though—
whoo—whoo—all aboard the train of
consciousness—I'll be your guide—don't hurt
me—now it may be dark but that'll change—
right now we're in a black hole—the
breathing maelstrom of repression—this
is where our fucked up host gets his
nasty thoughts—look closely—you

can see ‘em materializing—tears—
doctors—muffled cries—round pink
stomach explodes—hideous blood red
monster emerges from gaseous soul—
wearing a suit of bone fragments—
drooling marrow—her body shudders as it
slithers out and brushes her pale
vagina—
is she dead or desperate—
they vanish—
a cacophony of indescribable torture
and rainbow of a million colors
undulates—
our host—a manifestation appears—
blanketed in shadows—hides his left side
innocently—
this here if I’m not mistaken is his
worst fear—
whispers—
pay close attention as he steps into
the light—
plastic goat appears—our host slowly
approaches it—audible gasps—elderly Asian
lady passes out—
his body is black and decaying—cancer
visible like a swarm of June bugs—
eats his body from foot to chest—bones
inhale blood—he convulses in horror—juices
thick and black erupt from his
mouth—gums decay and teeth choke—cancers

spread like darkness—he screams—body crumples
and turns to dust—flowers rise from lonesome
grave—
beep—beep—
the time has come—expunge yer souls—let
yer innards roll—if you'd notice—under
yer seats're jars fer yer lung cookies—
fasten yer seat belts—put yer trays in
the upright positions—we are now journeying
to a mythical land—golden grains of
Tolkien—we will see our host's dreams—
the microbe sized shuttle shoots through
the canyons of our host—emitting nauseous
fumes—a winged hand falls from the heavens
and heads to its destination—
the skies—pure and gold—are home to silk
clouds and condescending rainbows—
countless eyes swim for the heavens and bleed
in tearful unity—
welcome—
cinematic clouds roll and rumble and rain a
million screenplays—shadows befall us as
our host pans down on slithering serpentine
crane and shoots us with electric eyes—
no pain here—he screams—cancer spreads
like darkness—no dreams from the grave—
this is boring—to move this story forward
our microbe sized train must derail—whoo—
whoo—I'll be your guide—don't hurt me—
expunge yer souls—candy coated jars fer

lung cookies—condescending home—pure and
gold—expunge yer cancer—like june bugs—
our host—gums choke—teeth decay—dreams—
nightmare—train—derails—elderly Asian
lady passes out

The day of the great tide came when I was a child—when
the sun rose and fell with great defeat into the abysmal waters
over the horizon—the moon is an old cliché dating back to
Sophocles—why must we trivialize nature in a pathetic attempt
to romanticize our idiosyncrasies—I am an old dirty whore who
fell from the graces of God—but no—I'm not—
still a virgin—believe that—still a lonely person—
though I'm twenty and thought—as a child—that no adults were
lonely—assumed everybody just met someone—didn't know the
hows or whys—didn't know of the laborious process of securing
a soul who would want to spend eternity with me—didn't know
anything—just the wonder and astonishment of witnessing the
sun slip into the sea—I'm not making sense—with whom am I
speaking—I remember a few years ago—just for kicks—we would
cut ourselves with extremely sharp knives—under the influence
of extremely dangerous drugs—all for the sake of masturbating
with our own blood—what joy it is to know that
those juices running down your leg is the legacy of ten
generations of decadent Irish men—I remember the day the earth
died—it got cancer from decades of nuclear testing—madmen
ran through the streets sodomizing themselves with butcher
knives—children sniffed gas fumes and snorted dried cum as
it trickled out of a clergy's withered old cock—I myself
was at home having sex with a gorgeous black woman who called
herself Cinderella because—well—I don't know why—but I tell

you this—that black beauty sucked cock like you wouldn't believe—I tell you boy—that bitch's pussy tasted like honey—felt like a moist vacuum cleaner—God I loved her—that is—of course—till that cocksucker tried to cut off my dick 'cause I was in love with her mother—who happened to be dead for six months—but that didn't stop me from tossing her salad every fucking night of the week—but anyway—I killed Cinderella and sold her to the local cannibals for a pack of cigarettes and seven ounces of opium—one time I fucked a sixteen year old hooker—she claimed to like it but she was just in it for the drugs—so I exploited her—cock pussy like honey—forced the whore to fuck the coffee table—lubed the leg with semen and saliva and fucked away—she cried harder than anything I'd ever heard—but deep down inside she liked it—heard her skin rip—a deluge of blood stained the table top—what a joy to watch various juices run down leg—sold salad tossing meat to cannibals—got lost and caught up on blood honey pussy opium—got lost on fucking young eager minded prostitutes—like fucking your daughter—young whore with fresh cunt—young whore fresh cunt—cried—deep down liked it—in it for drugs—her gardens fluttered—there is tossing her it—all that rhetorical her ethereal shadow sitting on rip—she cried—shut up you months—but that my lap—my children—I loved—didn't stop me from bloody bitch—fucked the immaculate moonlight—sold her to the local cannibals for honey—felt like a moist vacuum—a pack of linear insanity—bloody orgasms—skin cleaner—God cut off every fucking night of the dick 'cause fingers off yer bones—see—nothin week—but anyway—I killed Cinderella and sold to I that cocksucker sixteen year old hooker—she claimed to swam

in the dead ozone—click—flick—lick—roll like it but she was
salad those tried to but like honey cigarettes and seven ounces
mother—who happened to be dead from opium—one time I
fucked a six—that is—of course—till just in it for the was
in love with her bullshit drugs—so I exploited her needs—
cock pussy in the past is nothing—God is a sodomite—
tried to cut off my dick—dead six months—sold him to the
atheists for a carton of cigarettes and seven pounds of opium

She flows like wine—millennial movement—
moves across the room like an estranged spirit—
raises arms with seductive ease—cool white hair draped
over shoulders—plump breasts—nipples—naval—
looking down—rubbing moist crotch with dry finger—
"fuck me now"—dancing in orgasmic moonlight—
rubbing crotch—wet finger—"fuck me now"—
drapes over bed—rubbing nipple—sticks finger
in my mouth—tasty peach clitoris—
"fuck me now"—seeping skin—aroma—sex—cold
flesh against flesh—cock ripping pants—she forces
her tongue into my mouth—slits wrist—drips blood on
eager cock—ripping pants—lubes wet pussy with my
ancestors—"fuck—fuck—blood—breast—tastes wet crotch—
dry tongue—peach nipple clitoris—no more death—fuck—
fuck—worries—pain—moonlight orgasms"—she disappears—
lingering air—my children swim in the dead air—
orgasmic moonlight—what a sight—various juices run
down leg

The ocean swelled and collapsed on the shore as we sat on the beach watching stars dance through the void—I looked at my love—leaning back on her hands—and smiled—we'd been sitting there for hours—kissing and smoking the occasional joint without saying so much as a single word—she leaned forward and wiped sand from her palms—and flashed a smile on realizing I'd been watching her—she shifted her head to the left—questioning me—I smiled and pointed to a joint behind my ear—she nodded and presented her lighter—I lit it and took two hits—I handed it to her and picked splinters of weed off my tongue—her forearm slung back—the joint floated to her lips—I watched the hypnagogic orange cherry as she lit it—although we'd known each other for six months her beauty still amazed me—her long legs drew in and crashed at her waist—her lithe arms danced around—her smile revealed perfectly pearly white
teeth—her eyes—big and brown—narrowed—she tossed her curly jet black hair over her shoulder and passed me the joint—I smiled—the marijuana film coated my eyes—I tried to express my love for her but the words tripped over my tongue and crashed into my teeth—I fell forward with laughter—laughing she fell forward—clutching the sand—and crawled to me—writhing like a snake—I envisioned her as a giant cackling serpent devouring a desert and laughed harder—she planted her hands

on my knees and pulled herself up to me—I looked into her
eyes—our laughter faded—marijuana film coated eyes—lithe
arms—writhing snake—the ocean rose—collapsed on the
shore with laughter—I smiled—faded away—her tongue
fought through my lips and danced around my mouth—
we kissed for a century—she peeled herself away from me and
leaned into the sand—I leaned forward and—through marijuana
eyes—watched her finger her hair—her eyes swam
with the stars—I said I loved her—she didn't hear
me—I said it again—smiles faded—

Night haunts me with its realization of
sleep—of dreams—and with dreams—the
inevitability of your face dancing in
the void—the personification of
cowardice justifies my fear of
confrontation—your colors bleed through
my walls—I choke on its presence—I
am alone—wed to misery—shotgun wedding—
till death do us part—no matter how hard
I try I'll never divorce this lifelong
companion—but you've taught me that
something is out there—shown me the
fields over the horizons—
ah if only you could've shown me how
to harvest them—but they're out there—
I know that now—and in your antidote
the disease lingers—like your breath
on my tongue—and then you're gone—
gone—and as I look over—there is no
black mass obstructing my view of the
light seeping in through the door

I was walking down the street and saw a man carving
an elaborate tattoo on his face with a shard of
broken glass—what strange things one sees when he consumes
enormous amounts of chemicals—ah but it's okay—I've
my woman to back me up—the one I'm with now
has a bulldog named Chester—when he's lonely
she fucks him with a ceramic dildo while jerking
him off—she's a sick fucking bitch but gets
the best drugs—one time we were over her
brother Sico's house and she withdrew a large amount
of heroin from her purse—shot thirty cc's
into the tip of my dick—lonely sick bitch—fuckin'
dogs—I like to fuck her mouth when she tests me
to show her who the fucking boss is—strange things
I've named—walking under the neon blue
subterranean night—I throw lonely people to the
dogs and smoke their ashes in a rusty pipe—pathetic
cocksuckers weep at my feet—get a dick in their
ass and a gun in their mouth—nasty fuckin'
whores spread their dirty legs for smack—I
fuck 'em and tell 'em to go fuck themselves—
"ain't no lay that bad worth any kinda' cash"—
dirty fuckin' whore—I must admit—one time
I stumbled across a Vietnamese bitch who wanted
a quick fuck and quicker cash—slant eyed bitch

smelled like fish and spoke three words—"fuck me
now"—we were at my house—cockroach infested—
and she teased my cock with denim hand—howled at
the phosphorescent moon—rubbed vinegar on her
tiny titties—"fuck me now"—cockroach infested cunt—
stupid fuckin' whore killed herself in bathroom—
drinking drano—ripping asshole with dirty plunger—
smoke ash—rust pipe—hate—hate—morbid—pain—
masters of macabre—decadent monsters fuck
small children—drink gas—assault slant eyed
cockroach bitch with tattoo glass

The seeds of death conditions us for war—what
bastards with black hearts train wet behind the
ears soldiers to slaughter women and children—
cancerous hearts pump thick black oil blood—
osmosis severs synapses and
overloads brain with incestuous cravings for
blood—and rape—and death—twenty first
century mechanized soldiers running through
fluorescent pink sunset intent on raping
children with bloody barrel—march—march—
sweating blood—bleeding tears—angelic
silhouettes marching over sullen horizons—
coming into form—planting fiery seeds in
chest and head—harvesting dead gardens—
tombstones are planted where death grows—
death grows in treasonous political egos—
prophetic blood falls from sky—Jesus weeping
for innocent children—too scared to sacrifice
himself again—the first time was a fluke—
soldiers fail to hear—the stinging wisdom of
his tears—blood—rape—angelic seeds—planting
tombstones—death—death—morbid souls—
resurrect insurrection—kill the mind—release
the soul—mad political egos—bent on drinking
fresh blood from flesh grails—cacophonous air

raids—napalm—ground troops—march—march—
death—death—sweating blood—harvesting
tears—crooked soldiers smile—servicing
superiors with sexual favors—castrating innocent
townspeople—selling testicles as bubblegum—
fucking soft women who perform fellatio with
their dying breath—crying their children's names—
"O'! Holy Father—deliver me from madness—
death—death—release the soul—flesh sweat—
blood—death—soldier's milk stains my flesh—
can't describe—horror—death—blood—release—
God"—mad soldier with haunting eyes
bashes in skull to save bullets—
skull fragments crunch under military issue
boots like eggshells—death—blood—stains
flesh—mad political—desire—night's velvet
curtain closes for bloody first act—midnight
drama unfolds in proper dramatic context

I was once trapped inside a glass
sphere—
scared I began to
punch it—drowning in a
white
substance—
after countless punches I realized
that the sphere
was not
made of glass—but of an organic
substance—frantic—I continued to
punch it—and
realized that I was
trapped inside an
eyeball—
and the white substance was
damaged skull milk—
the

h r z n
o i o s

shimmered and
bubbled over—lights where
there was

darkness—
and realized that the
eye was tainted

Two silent soft spoken children walk hand in hand through an
empty nature preserve—the young boy looks at his female
companion and smiles at her—she looks up and realizes that
the leaves on the trees are nothing more than filters softening
the sun's blows—they look at each other and smile—
as the blue earth slowly
revolves around the
ancient sun
they age—before they realize it—they are madly in
love—the man looks at his female companion
and smiles at her—he's happy 'cause they're together—she
looks up and realizes that the sun is nothing more than a ball
of fire made to annoy the leaves in the trees—they look at
each other and frown—
as the blue earth slowly
revolves around the
ancient sun
they grow apart—the man looks at his female companion
and frowns because she has erected a wall between them—she
looks up and realizes that the sky prevents the sun from melting
the trees—they look at each other and smile

A fallible Saint entered a womb and sat in a booth below
a frozen waterfall—he withdrew a pack of playing cards
from his breast pocket and shuffled them—halfway through a
game of solitaire—he realized that the pictures had been rubbed
off the cards—he shrugged and finished his game of
bridge—looking up he saw a madman resting on the back of a
giant turtle shell—reading a Bible—wearing a shirt with
the Queen of Spades printed on its breast pocket—he rolled
a joint with a page from the Book of Revelations then paddled
his lily pad upstream—he came to shore a few feet away and
met a naïve young boy sitting on the beach picking slugs
from his feet—the Madman offered the joint—the Boy smiled and
accepted it—he took a few hits and chocked when he
realized he was smoking the Anti-Christ—he reached into
his turtle shell pouch and withdrew a joint rolled with a page
from the Book of Genesis—he smiled and handed it to the
Madman—he stood up and walked to the edge of the water—leaving
the Madman and the Garden of Eden behind him—Then he entered the
womb and joined the Saint in the booth below the crashing
wave—the Saint's eyes grew into large diamonds when he saw the
boy and realized that he could no longer play solitaire—and he
smiled when the boy withdrew a joint with a Queen of Spades
printed on it—

I.

There she sits—like an angelic goddess—soothing
you with her calm breath—immaculate flesh—and
in one timeless minute opens your eyes to all
you've taken for granted—all the trivial—
idiosyncratic gestures and visions you've
overlooked attacks you like a rabid dog and
shakes you from your slumber—but you ignore the
dreams because you've been without them for so
long—and would prefer to live in a world devoid
of passion and hope

II.

What nights you've spent weaving stories of
lovers taking your hand—leading you to never
never land—a world where you are loved and
acknowledged—where life is eternal and love is a
fruit that grows in forests—and the cold calm reality
sucks you into an empty room where the walls are your
companion—and your only friends are dreamers who've
been dead for generations—silent unrealistic songs
play in the background and instill in you a
sense of false hope—the only thread keeping you
afloat in these gloomy waters

III.

The hardest thing about life is knowing that it's not
eternal and wasting away without overcoming the hurdles
before you—without expressing your love—and living the
life you've envisioned without envisioning a new life
night after night—rotting with the rose securely placed
in your hand as you watch others give their flowers
away—but you can't rest—can't stop unless you are
certain you have what is yours—yet how can you be assured
when you refuse to grasp life by the throat and demand
it reveal its secrets—no I lied—the hardest thing about
life is waking up and realizing what you have is nothing
more than an illusion

Blood hungry Satyrs walk backward through liquid streets—
they watch the sky cry—and step in puddles of amphetamine—
backing against rippling dripping walls—once they noticed the
moon blink and set her many minions upon their battered
souls—the sun is a red beast bleeding LSD and PCP—and the
clouds are silk and cotton spiders languidly swimming toward
the spinning horizons—the flesh paved roads cater to ancient
crucified elders who curse the world with their disdainful
tongues—the monstrous forests grow ears and pulsating mouths—
and the sky has a gaping wound that has rained blood since the
dawn of civilization—blood stained fields dance to the
rhythm of night's music—recreating dramatic times—and
glorifying revolting massacres—and dementia penetrates
the fiery tunnels of our subconscious—expunging our spirits
and our souls from our hollow skulls—buildings grow from the
center of the planet like metal flowers—covering
the horizons with unfathomable chrome domes—and mechanized
eyes linger in all corners of the planet—scrutinizing free
will—abolishing individuality—liquid satellites swim in the
seas—penetrating the atmosphere—shooting radioactive arrows into
the bitter earth—
and tired hollow robots rush to obey a system that has destroyed
reason—and hope—and has persecuted those who've
questioned their status quo—fortunately the faceless spirits'll
return and question the robots and dying children of a

revolution that's grown cold—no more fetuses dripping
from diseased vaginas—no more hollow men catering to the rabid
dogs of eternity—no more blood hungry Satyrs postponing the
coming of dawn—no more worlds where words blast over the
precipice and ring in shallow soffits—no more worlds where the sun
refuses
to divorce the horizons—and denies us one more day to solidify
our loves—our lives—our love of life

I.

Sitting below the glass ocean—rotting—
empty flesh—weaving fists of greasy hair in
fits of blue rage—for all my wasted
time—I breathe false rhymes and force hope
into the mouths of eternal saviors

II.

Adnil is a word the Aztecs used to
describe a two faced—back stabbing—
plastic covered lying gossipy cunt

III.

I've seen her face a thousand times
and spoke words she'll never hear—standing
behind her counter—grinning—watching
me waste a small fortune on words I'll
never feel—can she see me—compulsively
buying these words to reach her—I smell
her innocence—and finally she gently
touches my hand and whispers those four
dreaded words—have a nice day—shit—
what'd I expect—she's doing her job—
pushing me out like everyone else—but
she smiles—she fucking smiles—does she

like it—torturing me like this—if only I
could get her to barter her emotions for
a few meaningless words—fuck—what'm I
saying—I'm stoned—can't think straight—
forcing the woman of my dreams into
prostitution—what'm I saying

IV.

Dreams introduced chaos into the collective
consciousness—chaos introduced
reality to the dreamer—reality and dreams
introduced rebellion—the birth of
complete awareness came when
man renounced the rose in his
hand and welcomed the surreality of
dreams

Reflection of love long lost—I lay on
the edge of my nineteenth birthday wondering—
O' wondering—where I went wrong—her face
shines in my mind's eye—reflecting—
I never gave her time to realize the love
I had—but no—I'll write—and as long as I write
the world will know the love we never
had—I feared showing you my heart—and I am
left alone to die inside—waiting for the
call that never comes—waiting—alone—
I fuck'd up—I love you

Earth is the pit of hell where the sun watches us with
his nefarious eye—where the people walk backwards
on sidewalks as New York big apple red blood flows
through the streets and into the sewers where it
breathes new life into the forgotten souls of
yesterday—and the moon is a god—displayed on
a brilliant night sky with a billion god like
manifestations watching over us—and the
demigods in the sky watch the breather of life with
a keen eye—our god—the tangible palpable creator of
all life—and who in turn watches us with his eye and spreads
radioactive monotonous rays
upon our morbid souls

Every once in a while—for no particular reason—I like to
imagine that I am a successful film director—and I'm loved
and cherished by everyone I know—I'm rich and famous—I
have everything—women want me—men envy me—I epitomize
success—in every aspect of my life—I have a nice
home—countless awards—everyone
recognizes me and whispers astonishment as
I pass them in a store or on the street—I am everything I hope to be—
Then my fantasy decays—and my dark side takes over—and
I plunge into a world of sex—drugs—liquor—death—my
darkest fantasies come to light—I become an angry—
belligerent person—denying all that has been given to me—
and when it gets too emotional—I erase the past—and emerge
as an aspiring wet behind the ears filmmaker—who just
sold his first screenplay—I rush out to tell my
friends—they are shocked because they were unaware
that I had an agent—let alone was finalizing a deal worth
hundreds of thousands of dollars—they are happy and we
celebrate—I meet a woman who wants me because I'm
successful—and later—upon startling realization that I'm
a good person—falls in love with me—and as I'm achieving
everything—I am pulled back to reality—and realize
that I have no money—no woman—no job—the only words whispered
behind my back are hateful—so I rely on
alcohol—drugs—and despair to alleviate the pain—and induce

a world where I can be another me

death is the fear
loneliness the disease
love the cure

once when I was young I thought myself invincible—nothing could
bother me—no one could penetrate my world—but then I grew
up and realized that I wasn't invincible—but a frail
lonely being—and I was constantly harassed and harangued by
thoughts—terrifying visions of death—then I craved love—
I searched in all the usual places and came up empty
handed—O' what do I do—what can I say—I'm alone and I'm
afraid to taste the dawn—I'm so complacent in total
darkness—when reality bites me with her sharpened teeth
I scream and run for cover—seeking only the finest of
poisons—like the deadly juices that took control of me just
a few hours ago—my friends and cousins were with me—it was
exhilarating—yet my mind wandered—pretended I wasn't alone—that
I had a woman—that she was beside me—drinking and laughing—I'd
look into the mirror and pretend she was beside me—then I'd
scrutinize my eyes and realize I'd never seen that
person before—that the coward looking back wasn't me—and
I continued to drink—to prolong the realization—
I can't bear the thought of being alone—and any moment
I think I'm not is fine by me

your haste—taste pain—distaste—black veins—
diamond studded gowns—purple rigor mortis veils—hungry
flesh—fresh wounds—lust borne scars—
the numbness drapes my flesh
like a meat fog—ominous air
stains hollow'd ground—
the taste of your haste brings
diamonds to my eyes
arms tattooed with breathing wounds—blood clogged
eyes—borne of distrust—thoughts and lust—
hooded mystics in the night—
your fear raises flesh with
cancerous fingers—hungry
teeth chew tainted meat
madmen asphyxiate on
the veins of the damned

sitting
alone
empty
alone
eating
alone
waiting
alone
sleeping
alone
writing
alone
thinking
alone
drinking
alone
smoking
alone
living
alone
dreaming
alone
dying
alone

alone—so alone—I've contemplated taking a knife to my stomach
and cutting out the fucking fist that continues to squeeze
it—it reminds me that I am alone—what the fuck is there left
for me to do—god forbid I find someone who'll accept me for
who I am—an empty—forlorn—tormented soul—and what does it
matter anyway—I've proven to myself time and again that I don't
want to be happy—remember Crystal—and Sandy—and Lindsey—
and all the other women I ran away from—shouting thousands
of excuses—and lamenting the death of happiness—and hope—
jesus christ—I wish I would befriend a mad fucking scientist
who would help me destroy my conscience—who could cut out the
cancer that is slowly taking my life—I sit here and rot—
dreaming of tomorrow—ignoring the fact that today is not
expendable—ignoring the fact that a woman will not grow from
the shadows and rescue me from oblivion—and why the fuck
do I write—what do I aim to
achieve—WHAT—WHAT—WHAT—what the fuck do I want—
what will it take to become the person I want to be—is
is too late—god I hope not—I don't want to be julius henry
for another fucking minute

When I was a child I liked to watch the
sunflowers dance in the breeze—liked to watch
the sun rise over the forest of roofs—
the way the breathtaking hues articulated the
random acts of violence—each hue in the morning
sky represented a different form of dementia—
but that was before the dawn of madness—
when insanity was considered a virtue—when
condoms grew pockets—and eyes reflected the
inertia of the lost soul—childhood was such a
pleasant experience—no worries—no loneliness—
no sleepless nights wondering when you're
going to die—just you and your innocence—
doing things only children do—then self
loathing kicks in—and you realize the extent
of your loneliness—realize the only things that
can comfort you are your loneliness—your misery—
your nightmares—your fears—O' what horrible
thoughts run through my melancholy head—random—dementia—
madness grew pockets—misery wanders the lonely
night—then total depraved decadent madness—chaos—
disorder—bloodless vampires consume the dead of night—
what demons enter stage right and take control of your once proud
and decent mind—mad thoughts erupt from dormant volcanoes—
parents ignore you—big brother blames music and movies—

and mad—insane—naked lunch—novels—and let you off the
hook—so why the fuck not continue with total mayhem till
state is under martial law—but it's all good anyway—
seeing how your loyal narrator here don't give no fuck—
give me rittalin—vicodin—uppers—downers—ludovico—
screamers—laughers—any fuckin thing you think you can
throw at me—I'm a fuckin Frankenstein monster that you
sons a bitches created—and you think you can bring me
down—you're wrong—ya see—there are more out there—
many more—and we're coming to get you—it's time to
kill the pussy ass—tree hugging—cocksucking
liberal system—this is the age of the apocalypse—
total destruction—anarchy—Armageddon—if this isn't the
last generation—I can't wait to see how decadent
the next one'll be—as a matter of fact—my
cock throbs at the thought of a generation of
degenerates completely free of conscience—because the day
will come when man succumbs to his own bleeding
wrists

I.

Night startles me with her paranoid laughter—
her cool calm children mock all who defy
the natural order of dreams—
her glassy eyes frighten me with
their uncompromising visions—
I am but a corpse waiting to be planted
in the eternal garden

II.

O' night—whose cynicism keeps my
tired feet planted on the frozen floor—
whose infernal doubt languishes in the dark
recesses of my mind—
whose devils rest on my shoulders
and coerce me into retaining the love
I have for another—
who chokes me with her silence and
pushes me out of an empty bed—
it is you—YOU

III.

Night—it is you who is mistaken—
in an hour—day—your natural enemy—
my savior—will rise over my left shoulder

and usurp your throne—
only then will my feet leave the floor—only
then will I be free

O' dear sweet love—for you I create immaculate
falsehoods with fickle words of wisdom—
a splintering manifestation of mindless
word abortions—
come taste the empty markings on these
tobacco stained fingers and know I mean well—
these words contain an infinitesimal amount of
metal—a hook meant to ripple your mirrored void—
I taste your perfume with infinite passion
and lure you with these words—
simple—terse prose accessible to
every denomination—
I paint superfluous portraits for you
to want and whisper—losing dreams of
comprehension—contradiction—
what dire roads I've traveled—the wind
interprets my empty footfalls as self-inflicted
wounds—no spontaneous revelations—
I am forced to travel
this dark alley and scoff at giddy raindrops
dancing in my presence—
exiled from this opulent palace—
like a lunatic lain to rest—
I've stripped myself of mortal
clothing—Newtonian inhibitions

pulling at me with the strength of a
thousand men—
alas—sweet angel—the epiphany came
too late—
for I've been dragged to the bleeding
hills and left to rot alone

This morning I woke
up laughing—ya believe
that—this morning *I* woke
up laughing—I can't imagine
what it could have been—
well, I've never woken in
a good mood before—wonder
what it could have been—
I don't quite know how to
take this—what could it've
been—hmm—this is quite a
mystery—I don't know what it
could have been but obviously
that slab of meat behind my
sleep fogged eyes thought it
quite funny—now allow me to
investigate this with complete
and total
            objectivity—
a few hours prior I woke up
startled—stifling dreams—
contemplating a reality in
which I finally came to terms
with my own mortality—a
terrifying world where the

demon clad eyes chased me
through the wilderness—I woke
up scared—then just a few
hours later I woke up
laughing—wonder what it
could've been—hmm—maybe
over the past couple days
I foolishly thought that I
had regained some innocence—
my dreams were proof of
that by exposing my paranoia—
and then I woke up laughing—
I woke up laughing—I woke up
thinking my problems were
over—I woke up thinking I
had changed

The clocks have stopped my
brother—time moves for
another—did you identify
the void as it wrapped
its cold claws around your
defenseless body—did you
know what was happening—
exhaled gunpowder breath as
eternal midnight penetrated
your stormy eyes—
—confrontation—
—howls—
—gunshots—
—warm summer concrete cradled
  the hands of eternity—
did you weep as stoic tears
soaked the earth—have you regrets—
realize all that you have done
wrong—did you enter the
void calmly—or fight like a madman
unable to contain his dementia—
'Los—with whom am I speaking—a
spirit or a corpse—you were
eighteen when the gods played
their cruel joke—eighteen—so

much ahead of—and behind you—
once younger I am now two years
your senior—and have experienced
that hot July morning two dozen
times—ah—you should have seen
it—the cold breath carrying
your news froze time—O' if ever
you thought yourself insignificant
you should've seen it—a million
eyes melted and married the swollen
earth—for you 'Los—for you—
if this is our only life I regret
losing touch with you—I regret
missing your funeral—but I couldn't
go—couldn't believe you were gone—
gone now—gone are your worries—
—incarceration—
—pain—
—paranoia—
—holding your breath for the
  phantom gunman—
but you were right 'Los—you were
right—he did come—pierced your
skin with stoic
bullets—and left you alone in
the middle of a desolate road—
screaming—crying—trying to
maintain your existence as
darkness enveloped you—
so much originality became a

cliché—and though after two
years you run
through a dozen heads—sleep—
sleep now my brother

Here I sit—hunched over a dirty
white desk—face parallel to the
cracked door—looking at the world
through the myriad wounds of my
heart—all forms of this planet manifest
themselves in my heart—I touch
its people with my soul—I interact with
terribly interesting people in my mind—I
live and work in my mind—it's the only time
I am truly confident—I love to sit on the
dewy balcony listening to nature's symphony—
watching the sun shoot across the sky
like a phosphorescent arrow—and pretend that
I am in another place—in another time—
in another mind—talking to the woman
I love—
but sitting in this quiet room—chanting
this mantra to my burdened walls—I writhe
and convulse when I realize that I have
no love—I was born—and will remain
julius henry—and he is all that I
have—
hugging myself—I sit and watch the
shadows dance across my walls and catch
glimpses of my own sad silhouette

as it hovers over this old dirty desk—mocking
me—realizing that this is how I will
look when the mortician closes the lid—
and now I wonder—am I all that I have—
has death been my companion all these
years—
I'm sitting here waiting to die—*wanting*
to die—giving this very minute to my silent
partner—trading my precious time warming up
to the object of my affection—but why—why—
how does this knowledge benefit me—it gives
me nothing more than longer nights—which is
exactly what I don't need—
I'm tired of lying in bed at night watching
the shadows devour the walls—I'm
tired of ghost writing my biography from the
grave—I'm tired of wondering if she likes
me—or if they'll accept me—I'm tired
of sitting in this gloomy plaster
tomb dreaming of the moment I'll be
free—

He sleeps alone—foolish—empty—color drained
from his flesh—
admiring blue television walls—
it's his
birthday—
so much life experienced thus far—
had a girl—
couple actually—nothing more than a kiss—
dreamt of it though—of sweaty flesh coalescing with
passion—
dreams of love and heartache—
can't shake his loathing—coward—can't shake the reality of
leaving a woman behind—barely knew her—could he know
her—could he open himself up to her—to let her heal his
wounds—for years he's dreamt of sweet relief—of holding
someone near—
but those dreams—
sweet friends—
have cleansed themselves like grind on rain swept asphalt—what
foolishness—who here dear friends would not steal a piece of
happiness from the unguarded cupboards of a stranger—
what a strange specimen we've stumbled upon—
what a lowly beast—
he cries—soaks pale sleeves with tears—his stomach writhes
in violent agony—invisible fists squeeze his gut as punishment

for his sins—
no intervention—
no goddess of the night—
no blonde angels tapping on his window—
no crystal eyes to taste his grief—
no flesh canyons—
no warm release—
he must pay—sweet friends—with the hand that firmly grasps
reality—with his nights—
with his days—
and lonely slave environments—
collect that taxable sweat—yon child—and think of dreams you've
left behind—
go ahead—
look through the window—
no sanctuary parked up the street—
no love—
no lust—
just rain sweeping the streets—
dirty blankets of the season—
do you think she'll return—
scoffs—
for *you*—
is she painting pictures of your soul—
do you think she's already forgotten—
is she lying in bed at two a.m. wondering what could have
been—does she know you're alive—does she—she's already
forgotten—
you've fucked yourself yet again—dear child—
don't show me those tears—

I don't care—
I'm here to study you—
everyone else is gone—
you've scared them away—
so it's just you and me—
no one to taste the salty pillow—no one to extinguish the
grief—
could've been—
possibly—
could've had a night of trust—
could've been set free—
but you fucked up again—sweet friend—wrapped in stained sheets
of callousness—ignoble—
scoffs—
coward—
don't think of her—
what's left but remnants of her smile—
you've corrupted the rest—like all the others—
what a lowly being—
what a strange specimen we've stumbled upon—
does Aaron dream of desire—or Mansfield in jail right now—
look at yourself—yon child—do you dare call yourself a
man—what significance does this day represent—
life—
joyous life—
for what have you to be thankful—
stop crying—no one to wash away those tears—
you fuckin coward—stay there—read the moans on the idiot
tube—you're sick—obese—a joke—no one hears your sobs—remove
those visions from your eyes—

don’t think of her—
quit torturing yourself you stupid bastard—
don’t look—
leap—
what purpose does reason serve when you’re stuck in the silence
of emptiness—
what conundrums I speak—
don’t think of her succulent smile—
her dream inducing eyes—
think of the nights you’ve spent alone—think of heartache—
your godless existence—what purpose have words served you—
don’t you wish you were but a casualty of passionless
educators—
what purpose do words serve—
go ahead—
slap yourself on the back—yon child—you’ve done good—
oh—and happy birthday to you

II.

The Image of Images

2003

I've always receded into that bright I'VE ALWAYS PRESIDED OVER another plane I'VE ALWAYS PRESIDED OVER another plane of existence; in a realm where of existence; in a realm where I was king; an award winning king; an award winning filmmaker; a visionary; an iconoclastic Poet. Filmmaker; a visionary; an iconoclastic Poet. Tell them what was on my mind. Was on my mind. Other people. I express myself to other people. I could not look a stranger in could not look a stranger in the eyes and tell them what my mind. I was certain that my mind. I was certain that I'd never posses the ability to I'd never posses the ability to express myself to before them frightened and intimidated me. I and intimidated me. I could never say what was on could never say what was on I've always receded into that bright world behind my eyes because the world behind my eyes because the one that existed before them frightened the one that existed

↔

The dual faces of an angel come into form on the side of a broken glass. They start out as twirling shadows—blinking hypnagogic eyes—then transform into a quasi-micro galaxy. Each star in this galaxy is a shattered emotion. The stars coalesce into a distorted face. The face slowly becomes a woman. Her synapses are constantly misfiring, which causes her three eyes to blink at random. Her face is as cracked as a sun-scorched desert. Her cheeks and forehead crack open whenever she tries to smile and reveals the atrophied muscles that hide beneath her skin. She is tired and disoriented. Her equilibrium was shattered upon her transformation, which causes uncontrollably violent shaking. She is temporarily mute. A rancid green liquid flows from her mouth whenever she tries to speak. It smells like decades old vomit. She scoops it up in her cupped hands and swallows it back down. She reminds me of someone but I can't quite figure out whom. Paragraph breaks are usually assigned arbitrarily for the sake of the readers, but play hell on this author tonight. She vomits again. This time it splatters against my leg. I lap some up with my finger and taste it. It tastes like pussy. She drops down on all fours and begins to bark like a dog. Shit explodes from her rotting anus and drips onto her bruised legs. She barks and retches. Dry heaves. Gasps. Moans. She speaks—"Your realization—7 p.m. on the dawn of midnight"—I laugh. She smiles. Her face cracks. Atrophied muscles. Hell on her three eyes. Quasi-micro transformation. Shit drips. Bruised legs. Tastes like pussy. "Midnight. Dawn of the on. 7 p.m. Your realization." I retch. She barks. Face vaguely familiar. Dual angel. I think she's a former lover distorted by memory. I laugh. "So this is what you've become?" She reaches out to me. I slap her hand away. Face cracks. I fuck her dry, bloodless wound. Her pores secrete my semen. I laugh. Former memory. Atrophied lover. "So this is what you've become"

↔

So I watch her discretely enough as to go unnoticed if she happens to glance up at me. sits there and thumbs through a magazine with Trent Reznor on the cover, and completely ignores me. Perhaps she's as uncomfortable as I am, I think. been a part of my dreams for so long and now that I'm alone with her she won't say a damn word to me. She just magazine. I stare at her and at the same time try not to look at her at all. It's a hard thing to do, though. She's it's too quiet in here for me. The only sound that fills the air is the occasional ffttt as she flips through the pages of her down at the ugly patch of brown carpet that separates us and imagine that it's a sand trap preventing me from being with her. I'm uncomfortable; so I'm sitting in Amity's apartment while she's stretched out on the couch across the room looking through a magazine. Her big green eyes are as fresh as ocean water and her thin, red lips are it was meant to conceal. Aside from that wonderful outfit, I get an eyeful of soft, pink flesh. Her shoulders slowly merge into her neck, which gives life that ends just above her breasts and looks as if she had to paint it on. It does a really good job of revealing every little detail that my eyes continue their northern ascent. She's wearing a black get-up; I don't know what it is. It's almost like a bustierre, or something. It's a black piece her legs. I can see a patch of silky flesh above her knees—and below her skirt—that are calling my name, but I can't answer them just yet. So plucked out of an old Bettie Page photograph. It definitely has antecedents in bondage and sadism. She's wearing long, black, heel boots that ride her shins halfway up Her outfit is quite striking tonight which makes it more difficult for me to look away. She's wearing a two-piece black number that looks like it was her beautiful face. Wonderland that's sitting beside the ashtray. that interesting to her and thumb through a copy of Alice's Adventure in back to her magazine. So I concede to the notion that I'm not at me, with an eyebrow raised, and I apologize. She smiles and goes I can only manage to push out a dry cough. She looks up So beautiful. I light a cigarette and attempt to say something—anything—but She's so beautiful as she sits there, I think.

There's no such thing as a happy ending in the really blood stream. But thoughts like those should be reserved for fairy tales be able to penetrate her soul and inject my love into her size of an atom. After that, I'd have no problems because I can't stumble upon a potion that could shrink me As I read a random passage I find myself wondering why because there's no real world. But be honest, I didn't have her in the first place. So I did what I had to, ya' see, because I could not get enough of her. Though, to again. It's been a while, ya' see, because I chose to isolate myself from her. Lot better in the flesh. I'm so happy that I finally get to see her I somehow managed to memorize every curve on her body and they look a whole I set the book aside and study her one more time. Even though I know it was without meaning, I must admit that I liked jokingly yelled at me for disappearing for six months then gave me a hug. she didn't seem to mind. In fact, she was happy to see me. She I must admit that it was pretty awkward showing up at her house, but to go out and get drunk that it isn't even funny. I've re-entered the land of the living and I'm so very extremely ready She finally drops her magazine and looks up at me. She stretches her lithe arms out as she yawns. I yawn too, and tell her to knock it off. Her bored eyes expand in a gesture that seems to say '*so*'. I raise my eyebrows and project the same sentiment. Don't you hate it when you become friends with someone you want really good to see you again, Dylan. We all missed you." I just "I hear that," I say. She smiles at me. "It's "Well," she says. "You know how he is. He'll get here when he does." I say. "He just told me to meet up with you over here." "What time is he supposed to be here?" She asks. "Not sure," Don't you hate

Don't you hate it when you become friends with it when you become friends with someone you want to love? want to love?

↔

Explode in your head—don't hold back— explode in your head—don't hold back— me—I hold cancer but liquid words excite me—I hold cancer like vodka—see—and uncontrolled visions of bloody orgasms like vodka—see—and uncontrolled visions of bloody orgasms you like black cancerous fists—and eyeballs are cinematic windows—all words are mere words eyeballs are cinematic windows—all words are mere words but liquid words laugh at your satire—your emptiness is open—brutal—laugh at your satire—your emptiness is open—brutal honesty grips you like black cancerous fists—and honesty grips of meat our buried pasts—the soaring fountains of meat and blood—where words flow like water—the cacklin jackals and blood—where words flow like water—the cacklin jackals of a new form of literature— witness the rotting corpses of literature— witness the rotting corpses of our buried pasts—the soaring fountains—I am a man—I am a I am a man—I am a god—witness the birth of a new form god—witness the birth

↔

I've seen it with my own two eyes. It with my own two eyes. I'm staring at it now while I'm staring at it now while she punches in the codes for she punches in the codes for the last song, and it's the last song, and it's a wonderful feeling. It's the type of wonderful feeling. It's the type of feeling that I want to nurture feeling that I want to nurture until it can no longer be until it can no longer be contained inside me. And contained inside me. And to the moment we give in to our demons and neglect the present. our demons and neglect the present. And that, my friends, is a…And that, my friends, is a crime greater than murder. To neglect crime greater than murder. To neglect the present is to neglect your present is to neglect your passion, your potential, your life, and passion, your potential, your life, and your desires. Only then will you be your desires. Only then will you be a bitter fuck who thinks be a bitter fuck who thinks happiness is a fluke. But its happiness is a fluke. But it's not—believe me it isn't—because I've seen it is you forever. Only when it is handed to you will it feel handed to you will it feel temporary and intangible. The only way temporary and intangible. The only way for one to truly earn it for one to truly earn it is to forget about one's past is to forget about one's past and forge ahead. The past has and forges ahead. The past has its place and that's behind us. Its place and that's behind us. The minute we begin to blame The minute we begin to blame our problems on the past is our problems on the past is the moment we give in a fleeting abstraction that happiness is a fleeting abstraction that can never be obtained. If that can never be obtained. If obtained, it is quickly lost. And obtained, it is quickly lost. And that's a terrible stance to take. That's a terrible stance to take. Only Martyr's and Eunuchs do so Only Martyr's and Eunuchs do so and they are fools for it. And they are fools for it. Happiness is something that's earned not Happiness is something that's earned not acquired. If you earn your happiness acquired. If you earn your happiness then those feelings will stay with then those feelings will stay with you forever. Only when most people, including Joe realizes this. Most people, including Joe and Stephen, just think that she's and Stephen, just think that she's a bitter, opinionated chick who will be a bitter, opinionated chick who will never be truly happy because she never be truly happy because she doesn't want to be happy. But doesn't want to be happy. But I disagree. She does want to I disagree. She does want to be happy—I think she yearns for to be happy—I think she yearns for happiness—but years of being tuned out happiness—but years of being tuned out and mislead have left her fearful and mislead have left her fearful that happiness is it nonetheless. Perhaps I'm the see it nonetheless. Perhaps I'm the only person who does see it—I'm only person who does see it—I'm not fully convinced that she does—and not fully convinced that she does—and that makes me as sad as that makes me as sad as the thought of not being with the thought of not being with her. I'm convinced that she's the her. I'm convinced that she's the greatest person on the face of greatest person on the face of the planet and it saddens me the planet and it saddens me that I'm the only person who that I'm the only person who realizes this. She is such She is such a terrific person, the type of a terrific person, and the type of woman that I've always dreamt of. Woman that I've always dreamt of. She's incredibly intelligent, quick-witted, hip, likes She's incredibly intelligent, quick-witted, hip, likes all the things I like—music, books, all the things I like—music, books, movies, you name it—and has movies, you name it—and has a heart as big as mine. Although heart as big as mine. Although that heart has been hidden behind that heart has been hidden behind years of neglect and mistreatment, years of neglect and mistreatment, I see

↔

He stands on his scarred feet with renewed interest and the wounds on his ravaged flesh seal up before his very eyes while hope is reborn in its reflection so he walks over the harmless glass and discovers a broom that's been hiding in the shadows landing beside a giant pile of glass, where he gets a better understanding of what it's like to be left to your own devices after all, the glass was merely sand that never even asked to be transformed a billion grains can filter through your fingers without ever getting hung up whereas a sheet of glass only reflects the face that stares down a broom in hand but children and fairy tales hold the exclusive rights to magic he grows older as he waits for his ethereal lover to move through the century and offers god his soul in exchange for one night to help her clean it up neither of them ever arrive so he finally gives in to his pain and collapses on the floor, women with diamond eyes produce finer cuts he tries to disarm them before they make their move and is hurt worse in the process his bruised arms are a testament to his slow actions so he tip-toes through his own house while he waits for someone to come and clean it up, assuming that a stranger will come along with piece this puzzle back together would negate his regression so he stumbles through his house with bandaged feet and a crippled soul cursing his ignorance every time he changes the blood soaked gauze which is more frequent because the mess accumulates with each growing day he meets a new person who tosses a fresh sheet on the floor then laughs when he can't accepted this mess as payment for a life not lived and tears apart his soles whenever he forgets to look where he's going he's the one eyed ruler of this blind kingdom every now and then he sits on the corner of his bed and stares down at the melancholy vortex that blankets his solitude and contemplates cleaning it up but an attempt to Of memories and regrets A shattered sheet of glass is stretched across a broken floor each shard represents regret in a man's life time that's been melted and laid to waste this mosaic of tears paints portraits that he'd soon forget but passion and nonsense has forbidden him from sweeping this mess up and his thoughtful carpet has refused sanctuary to another broken memory

↔

I mean the bitch disgusted everyone. I can't even define what it was about her that nauseated me but everyone else in the deli felt it as there aren't many people that I honestly loathe but this chick really set the standard for everyone who followed after her. the old deli that I worked at and spent countless hours talking about her miserable life to whomever would listen. Now like she was storing phlegm in her cheeks and she wobbled like a discombobulated penguin. She was a fellow employee at head, a long neck, and a body completely devoid of definition. She talked with a wet lisp that made her sound I once knew a chick that was shaped like a bowling pin. I kid you not.

↔

Anybody can make cut-ups. It is three. And you have a new page. The method is simple. Here tasting sounds smelling forms. his color of vowels. And his "systematic derangement of the senses." The place of mescaline hallucination: seeing smell images to sound sight to sound sound to kinesthetic. This is where Rimbaud was going with into writing enabling the writer to turn images in cinematic variation. meaning for the cutter. Table tapping? Perhaps. Certainly an definite. Take any poet or writer you fancy. Here, say, or poems in their words. Cut the word lines and you will hear their voices. Cut- ups often come would fall twice as fast. It did not occur to them to push the two objects off the table and see how write now. Not something to talk and argue about. Greek philosophers assumed logically that an object twice as heavy as another object Cut-ups movie or still cameras the middle. You have four sections: are by The cut-up method brings 1 2 3 Assured of good to writers the collage, which has poetry at least if not personal been used by painters for seventy appearance. contacted poets through a medium. years. dimension of scissors renders the Rimbaud announces himself, to be followed process explicit and subject to extension by some excruciatingly bad poetry. Cut and Rimbaud's words and you are through as code messages with special The best writings Now rearrange the sections placing section seems to be done almost by four with section one and section the unpredicatble factors of passersby and two with section Cutupis for everyone." juxtapositon cut-ups. And photographers will tell Poetry is a place and it you that often their best shots is free to is one way are used by the moving and to do it. Take a page. still camera. In fact all street Like this page. Now cut down shots from accident but years of repetition. Now Sometimes it writers until the cut-up method was says much the same thing. Sometimes made explicit-all writing is in fact something quite different-cutting up political speeches cut-ups; I will return to accidents is an interesting excercise-in any case . . . experimental in the you will find that it says sense of bein something to do. something and something quite 4 . Right here colors writers will tell . . one two three four. you the same. writing poem and type out selected passages. is in fact cut-ups. A collage Fill a page with excerpts. Now of words read heard overheard. What cut the page. You have a else? unpredictable spontaneous factor with a new poem. As many poems as pair of scissors. this point-had no you like. As many you have way to produce the accident of read over many times. The words spontaneity. You cannot will spontaneity. But have lost meaning and life through you can introduce the all cut up Rimbaud and you Images shift sense under the scissors are in Rimbaud's place. Shakespeare Rimbaud composed entirely of rearranged cut-ups. Cutting poems as you like. Tristan Tzara and rearranging a page of written said: "Poetry is for everyone." And words introduces a new improvement on Andre Breton called him a cop the usual deplorable performances of they and expelled him from the movement. fall. Shakespeare Rimbaud live variation. Clear Say it again: "Poetry take the classical prose can be All for everyone.

↔

remnants of peach clitoris her finger in my over bed—rubbing nipple—sticks her finger in my mouth—tasty remnants of peach clitoris mouth—tasty orgasmic moonlight— rubbing crotch—wet finger—“fuck me now”— drapes orgasmic moonlight— rubbing crotch—wet finger—“fuck me now”— drapes over bed—rubbing nipple—sticks down—rubbing moist crotch with dry finger— “fuck me now”—dancing in with dry finger— “fuck me now”—dancing in arms with seductive ease—cool white hair draped over shoulders—plump breast—nipple—naval— looking down—rubbing moist crotch draped over shoulders—plump breast—nipple—naval— looking an estranged spirit— raises the room like an estranged spirit— raises arms with seductive ease—cool white hair She flows like wine—millennial movement— moves across She flows like wine—millennial movement— moves across the room like

↔

make any sense...I just need some help because I'm afraid that I'm going to do something really stupid in a time of need...which is often because no one could possibly imagine what I go through when I am by myself...and I've been alone a lot lately...but...well, I'll shut up now...and I'm sorry... D. kills me...because she promised me that she wouldn't write me off...I know where her life's going and I fear that she will never give me the opportunity to make up for what I've done...and it kills me...I just have a million things sitting on my mind right now...sorry that I keep bringing her up but she is really my only tangible problem--if to help me--aside from you, that is...and you are my friend, I know that, and I was never talking to you to be close to her...you're my friend and I appreciate your friendship...I also appreciated your sisters friendship but I went and fucked that up really really badly...I fear that I will never hear from her nor see her again and that to do about it...I don't know what to do...I don't hear from most of my friends anymore and I honestly have no idea why, I never said or did anything to them...no one calls me anymore nor does anyone--aside from you--talk to me via yahoo messanger...I'm so hurt and alone right now and I need help but I don't think anyone wants suicide were hanging on my mind...so I vented all of my fears and aggressions on her...I don't know what's wrong with me, I don't...she does factor in to this but I don't know to what degree anymore...it just feels like the whole world is against me...I feel like I'm the only person in this fucking town right now...and I don't know what scared the fuck outta' me...so here I am today...alone, broken, and scared...I'm trying to finish this fuckin' book 'cause I'm gonna' try to get it published after I re-write it a couple of times...I didn't mean anything that I said about your sister the last time we talked but my head was so fucked up then...I was so depressed and thoughts of I wasn't avoiding you and it has nothing to do with you...but I think I need some help, I think I need some real help...I'm so very extremely fucked up right now and I don't fully understand why...ya' see, my nights are so dark and miserable that I'm driving myself insane...I came frighteningly close to killing myself last night and it no longer exists...I'm just gonna sit here and wait for my eventual end...nice knowing ya being a vague memory to them...but whatever...I might as well get used to this numbness...and don't bother responding...cause godofmovies and julius, from this moment forward, no that was born to suffer...I really really really dont wanna live anymore...and the three kids are the only reason I haven't killed myself...I don't intend on just sit here and cross my fuckin fingers that I get cancer or something...then I'll be free of everything that haunts me...namely, julius henry, the bastard gonna do cause I just plan on sitting here and suffering...cause apparantly thats my lot in life and I might as well get used to it...I'll hate myself...bad...real bad...like I get pissed that I even fuckin wake up in the morning...so don't bother to get ahold of me to see what I'm dude, seriously, not only am I never going out again...but I'm not even gonna talk to anyone again...I fuckin hate the world

↔

número de "corte" y "dado" o número de "corte" y "dado" o puedes seleccionar la opción de "nuevo" puedes seleccionar la opción de "nuevo" para trabajar con un texto distinto. para trabajar con un texto distinto. procesador de palabras, de o de procesador de palabras, de modo que puedas guardarlo si lo modo que puedas guardarlo si lo deseas. Luego puedes volver a los deseas. Luego puedes volver a los mismos textos para reformarlos con otro mismos textos para reformarlos con otro ser reformado. es cortado antes de ser reformado. Una vez que obtengas el nuevo Una vez que obtengas el nuevo texto, puedes copiarlo (copy) y pegarlo texto, puedes copiarlo (copy) y pegarlo (paste) en un documento de texto (paste) en un documento de texto o de que dice "cut-up". También puedes experimentar con distintos valores de "dado" y con distintos valores de "dado" y "corte", que alterarán el número de "corte", que alterarán el número de partes en las que el texto partes en las que el texto es cortado antes de palabras que han sido insertadas. Escribe o pega un texto insertadas. Escribe o pega un texto en las áreas que se encuentran en las áreas que se encuentran aquí abajo y presiona el botón aquí abajo y presiona el botón que dice "cut-up". También puedes experimentar propio trabajo. El cut-up funciona bajo principios similares El cut-up funciona bajo principios similares a los del collage y el a los del collage y el montaje fotográfico; crea una nueva imagen montaje fotográfico; crea una nueva imagen de las palabras que han sido de las Esta es una máquina de cut-up Esta es una máquina de cut-up que trabaja mediante principios similares a que trabaja mediante principios similares a los utilizados por William Burroughs y los utilizados por William Burroughs y Brion Gysin en su propio trabajo. Brion Gysin en su

↔

Ultimately, 18 schools developed, each with their own interpretations developed, each with their own interpretations of various issues, and spread all of various issues, and spread all over India and Southeast Asia. over India and Southeast Asia. Today, only the school stemming from Today, only the school stemming from the Sri Lankan Theravadan survives. the Sri Lankan Theravadan survives. philosophical developed a complex set of philosophical ideas beyond those elucidated by Buddha. ideas beyond those elucidated by Buddha. These were collected into the These were collected into the Abhidharma or "higher teachings." But Abhidharma or "higher teachings." But they, too, encouraged disagreements, so that they, too, encouraged disagreements, so that one splinter group after another left one splinter group after another left the fold. Ultimately, 18 schools -- "the labeled themselves the Mahasangha -- "the great sangha." They would eventually great sangha." They would eventually evolve into the Mahayana tradition of evolve into the Mahayana tradition of northern Asia. The traditionalists, now referred northern Asia. The traditionalists, now referred to as Sthaviravada or "way of to as Sthaviravada or "way of the elders" (or, in Pali, Theravada), the elders" (or, in Pali, Theravada), developed a complex set of fragment. The most Buddhism began to fragment. The most significant split occurred after the second significant split occurred after the second council, held at Vaishali 100 years council, held at Vaishali 100 years after the first. After debates after the first. After debates between a more liberal group and between a more liberal group and traditionalists, the liberal group left and traditionalists, the liberal group left and labeled themselves the Mahasangha be translated into the monks, to be translated into the many languages of the Indian plains. many languages of the Indian plains. It should be noted that It should be noted that Buddhism remained an oral tradition for Buddhism remained an oral tradition for over 200 years. In the next over 200 years. In the next few centuries, the original unity of few centuries, the original unity of Buddhism began to and favorite disciple -- and friend, and favorite disciple -- and a man of prodigious memory! -- a man of prodigious memory! -- recited Buddha's lessons (the Sutras). recited Buddha's lessons (the Sutras). The monks debated details and voted The monks debated details and voted on final versions. These were on final versions. These were then committed to memory by other then committed to memory by other monks, to Soon after Buddha's death or parinirvana, Soon after Buddha's death or parinirvana, five hundred monks met at the five hundred monks met at the first council at Rajagrha, under the first council at Rajagrha, under the leadership of Kashyapa. Upali recited leadership of Kashyapa. Upali recited the monastic code (Vinaya) as he the monastic code (Vinaya) as he remembered it. Ananda, Buddha's cousin, remembered it. Ananda, Buddha's cousin, friend

↔

haunts me with its realization Night haunts me with its realization of haunts me with its realization of sleep—of dreams—and with dreams—the inevitability of sleep—of dreams—and with dreams—the inevitability of of sleep—of dreams—and with dreams—the inevitability of sleep—of dreams—and with dreams—the inevitability of your face dancing in the of your face dancing in the void—the personification your face void—the personification your face of of cowardice justifies my fear of confrontation—your colors of cowardice justifies my confrontation—your colors of cowardice justifies my fear of confrontation—your colors bleed through fear of confrontation—your colors bleed through my walls—I choke on its bleed my walls—I choke on its bleed through my walls—I choke on its through my walls—I choke on its presence—I am alone—wed to misery—shotgun Night presence—I am alone—wed to misery—shotgun Night haunts me with its realization Night us part—no wedding— till death do us part—no matter how hard I do us matter how hard I do us part—no matter how hard I try—I'll part—no matter how hard I try—I'll never divorce this lifelong companion—but you've never divorce this lifelong companion—but you've try—I'll never divorce this lifelong companion—but try—I'll never divorce this lifelong companion—but you've dancing in the void—the personification you've dancing in the void—the personification of cowardice justifies my fear there—shown me the something is out there—shown me the golden fields just over the me golden fields just over the me the golden fields just over the the golden fields just over the horizons— ah if only you could've horizons— ah if only you could've shown horizons— ah if wedding— till shown horizons— ah if wedding— till death presence—I am alone—wed to misery—shotgun death presence—I am alone—wed to misery—shotgun wedding— till death do to harvest them—but they're me how to harvest them—but they're out there— I know that now—and out there— I know that now—and in your there— I know that in your there— I know that now—and in your antidote the disease now—and in your antidote the disease lingers—like your taught me that something lingers—like your taught me that something is out there—shown taught me that is out there—shown taught me that something is out gone—and as I tongue—and then gone— gone—and as I tongue—and then you're gone— gone—and as I look you're gone— gone—and as I look over—there is no black mass obstructing over—there is no black mass obstructing look over—there is no black mass look over—there is no black mass obstructing only you could've shown me obstructing only you could've shown me how to harvest them—but they're out how to harvest them—but they're out me how my view of the light that my view of the light that seeps my view of the light seeps my view of the light that seeps in through the door that seeps in through the door in through the door breath on in through the door breath on my antidote the disease lingers—like your my antidote the disease lingers—like your breath on my tongue—and then you're breath on my tongue—and then you're gone—

↔

A blistered candle dances
On my lap like hot wax
The memory of her melts and
Runs down my neck
My face begins to play back
And runs
Silent as my mind widows me
And her eyes envelop oblivion
Misery obscures my vision
She glances up at a veil
She takes a warm smile and wing of
An angel plucked from the
Feather of her arm
Amity
Amity at the bar
Lying in wonderland
Fuck me
Her warm snatch slides
Into my finger
We lay in the room of her
Bed
Cold tears
Sweaty thighs
Salt
Bedroom

Lies

The door opens

I lay

Down

↔

The bedroom walls cackled at my cowardice. She bit my neck, tried to draw blood but I wanted her to taste a different juice. Her cold body clung to my sweaty chest. She grunted and punched my head. I ran my finger along the wall. I cut myself on her coarse bush. Her juices ran down my forearm. I bit her sweaty thigh. The salt made my cock rock hard. She moaned. Juices boiled. She bit my neck. I bit back and ran my finger along her cracked bush. She grunted and cowered. The salt made her punch my forearm. Syntax. Grammar. Cold moonlight. Moist finger. Arbitrary paragraph. Continued.

↔

People get data angel come into nations in the middle of a broken glass. American weapons…war…twirling shadows—blinking part of a plot has nuclear transforms into audiotape reportedly from…in this galaxy, each Korea could possess such emotions. The Korea's outgoing President's distorted face. Her cooperation by U.N. why misfiring, which Korea focus attention…three eyes to blink from the north came is as cracked as a President George W….her cheeks and forehead the Brussels meeting…he tries to smile policy will flutter like atrophied muscles that in the nuclear conflict skin. She is tired…huge global winters…equilibrium was shattered…a landscape…a character…which causes 7 numero de "corte" y shaking. She is temporarily de "corte" y "dado" O' green liquid flows from la opcion de "Nuevo" parades old vomit. She texto disinto. Para cupped hands and texto disinto. Procesadun. O de procesador de me of someone but que puedas guardarlo my finger on her. Paragraph puedas guardarlo si assigned arbitrarily.

↔

Deaths. Snarling traffic, closing airports and schools and causing at least a dozen than 2 feet of snow—Homeland Security Secretary Tom Ridge. Storm buried some areas with paranoia sometime in the near future, says in hand after a massive winters its current high-risk, or orange, status spent President's Day weekend with shovels level will probably be lowered from millions of people across East Washington—the current terrorism threat on Friday. Photogenic Bear! Her boyfriend, who had just eaten a few shrimp, doctors reported away or dodging it into severe anaphylactic shock after kissing a burrow. This is one but they often avoid fighting predators 20-year-old woman with shellfish allergies went by running you have large shovel-shaped heads, warthogs look fierce, food allergies. A kiss is not the weird age with four tusks and just a kiss. Here's a tale to dampen romantic tropical islands: sometimes a kiss slowly moves into passion so that they come back as something better. You get bad karma and may suffer in your next life. People who believe in reincarnation often work to be a good king?—this is called karma. You get good karma from being a kind and loving person. If you are cruel, you are good a state court said on Friday or bad will determine what you come back as (a crow? A pair of bull castration tongs of Hinduism and Buddhism). Both religions in the western town of Duesseldorf, believe that whether years in jail a different body. This belief is attacking a factory worker with an important part of the religions. Reincarnation is the belief that after a lovesick 58-year-old German has died, we come back in sentences of seven.

↔

The city is an old tired junky. Stoned on immigrants. They fall from the heavens and trip over its citizens. The citizens go on with their daily routines and assassinate the fear in their owner's faces. An airplane explodes. Epiphanies and lost dreams rain down on the cities inhabitants. They run—screaming and crying—trying to escape a growing cloud of depression. The sky is split open and bleeds on the cities native children. A tablecloth dances in the breeze. Four soldiers carry a decadent priest through the desolate streets. He's feigning exhaustion. God blinked and missed his ruse. "Tomorrow. Baghdad. News. Inside. Confused. Adolescent. Scared. Tattoo. Terrified. Crumbled. Lost. 3500. Dead." A rotting arm waits on a rooftop for someone to shake its hand. Death retires in 18 months to spruce up the value of your home. Looking at the viability of cable activity. Email. Rally. Blizzard buries E. Coast. Immigrants. Raining down. Afraid. Assassinates the stoned city. God blinked and tripped over its faces. The sky dances in the decadent streets. Adolescent. Dead. Scared. A rotting priest waited on God.

↔

Birth. Transcendental rainbow seizes the oxymoron of expression. The sun: Birthright of a lasting culture. The city is old, has been washed up for eons. The buildings remind me of a withered fetus that was never removed from the womb. Its windows reflect the misery of its tenant's souls. They leak smack and piss depression. I fucked a widow. She came in my face. Squirted like a goddamned geyser. I didn't mind, though, 'cause I poured her juices into her mongoloid son's cereal. Gave back to the earth. The earth is a wound on God's Achilles heal. He cut it when he was walking through the Garden of Eden. He wanted to kill Eve. The cunt. She learned more than he did. He couldn't have that. But she avoided him. He zigged when he should've zagged. He got pissed and left mankind to his own incompetence

↔

"The thing itself—WS Burroughs the thing itself—WS Burroughs mind and not of the image of images of words repeated in the become images when written down, but become images when written down, but are and how they function. They are and how they function. We must find out what words. We must find out what words become images when written down."

↔

I have to tell you that for you, the refined public, I don't have the equivalent of a leper. But I chastise the general public in a manner of speaking. When these Dadaist's are close to you they treat you with that remnant of elegance some people get. "Data power to attack Muslim nations in the Middle East stupid." And claims American weapons...war plans against Iraq are part of a plot of the nuclear inspectors. An audiotape reportedly from Osama weapons, South Korea could possess such bin Laden as South Korea's outgoing President warned Bush Iraqi cooperation by U.N. weapons that if North Korea focus attention again on the bluster from the north came the rift between President George W. red flag anti-war protests, the Brussels meeting is of the army-first policy will flutter likely too. "The victory in the nuclear conflict after a weekend of huge global winters is ours. And the lake, a landscape, a character."

↔

To construct a frame of reference, the face of such complexity, escapes into specialization and parochial narrowness. Into specialization and parochial narrowness. As it does with processes, which are, it does with processes, which are ever changing. Little wonder that Psychologists aren't ever changing. Little wonder that Psychologists, in the face of such complexity, escape the species, the current status of the species. Most difficult of all, most, most difficult of all, the scope of psychology is complex, dealing with the history of his ancestors, back through the evolutionary vicissitudes and triumphs which have determined vicissitudes and triumphs which have determined the current status of its long experience; and it is long—tracing back through the history of tracing back through the history of the individual, through the history of the individual, through non-conscious. The scope of study is broad—covering the study is broad—covering the infinite variety of human activity and experience; and psychology is the systematic attempt to describe, psychology is the systematic attempt to describe man's conscious and non-conscious scope of behavior: Conscious and non-conscious scope of behavior.

↔

Her undefined face is so tight that I can feel the flesh beneath it. Steal a bit of her warmth. Her bustierre, or whatever it is, around her body, I squeeze in a magazine. Amity. Amity. Amity. Amity. Amity. Amity. Amity. Amity. Amity an attempt to face. With my arms still wrapped across the room looking through Amity. So I'm sitting in Amity's apartment and close my eyes. A slight smile dances across my face.

↔

but i guess no one cares anymore because no one will listen to me nor will they respond. but these feelings are real and i wanted to address them once and for all. it all right. that's not going to happen, however. i'm still me and he is alone but don't fret because i'm almost done with the julius we all know. i just wanted to say that these feelings are still here and they're not going away. have been given. i love you. I don't know why but i do. and this feeling that rests in the pit of my stomach will be here for quite some time. i just wish that i could do everything over again so i could do blew up in my face. i just wish that i was in your arms right now because i have so much to give--so much to give--but you don't want it because i'm a spineless little freak who didn't give you the attention that you should been anyone but me, but i'm not and i waste away like i always do 'cause i'm too scared to do anything until it's too late. i wrote that book to show you how much i felt for you but i fucked up and it i have this empty feeling in the pit of my stomach that keeps shouting your name and i can't shut it up. and i sit here and suffer because i am me. and i think that we could genuinely have been good together had i hey, i know you're sick of hearing from me but i'm just sitting here and need to say that i still have incredibly strong feelings for you and can't stop thinking about you though i don't know why. but i wanted to say this because everyone will just forget what I've done and that we all can go back to how we were before. So this is the last 'serious' or 'heavy' email you'll recieve from me 'cause I've gotta' learn to let things be. them. I still have these feelings that I'm trying to hard to escape from but I guess only time can kill them off. Lord knows I've tried--and failed miserably. But anyhoo. I'm just so very extremely sorry for being such a dickhead lately and hope to be done about it, nothing. not that i'm insunuating anything's gonna' go down but, hey, I do have an active imagination and there's nothing I can do about this whole N.C. thing. There are somethings that a spineless coward such as I have to live with and this is one of just one more act of cowardice that I'll have to live with. But anyhoo. True, I still have feelings for you that will probably not disappear anytime soon, and it's be eaten me up to learn that you're going down there for two days in feb. but's what let me just say that I'm sorry for being such a melodramatic bastard. I lost sight of what was important to me because I thought I'd lost everything. So blah, blah, wolf, wolf, and all that jazz. I wanted to kill myself but didn't hav the balls to do it so that's apologized to. If the term 'friend' is still appropriate because--even though you've denied it--it just seems to me that you go out of your way not to speak with me. But anyhoo. I'm not trying to start anything, I'm only trying to resolve everything. Now. Right here. So Ya' know what? Not that you care but I know I've been a really, real big cocksucker lately and now fully understand the depths of my ignorance. I'm only sending you this email because I never see or talk to you anymore and you're the only friend that I haven't formallyI'm drunk so pardon, but I think I really need to talk to you. We need to talk. There are things I need to say...and probably things I don't wanna' hear but I know there are things you need to say. I'm so alone and I hurt so much but I need to know what's going on. Although I think it's fairly obvious. I don't wanna' hear it but I'm sure I need to. I just...I need to talk to you...I need to see you without excuses...I want to know a few things...like what is it about me that's so repulsive...the last two women I told I liked--Emily and Dawn--just completely skipped town and I sense you're gonna'...hell, you already said you're gonna' go down to north carolina in late january--which is around my birthday so that's very fuckin' fitting00but whatever,,,I just wanna' know what's wrong with me...I can read bewtween the lines nonetheless...yout aloofness hasdn't gone unnoticed...but whatever...I wanna' talk to you...I don't get the chance to when we're out...although I really, really wanted to tonight...but I'd really like to talk to you...face to face...I'm supposed to go out with joehn and nick tomorrow--friday--but I'll sell them out because I'd rather talk to you...so please gfet ahold of me...via email, telephone, or yahoo messenger but I wanna' talk...please....oh., and I apololgize for the terrible spelling but as I said I'm pretty fuckin wasted rtight nowbut can we talk...cause I hate looking at you as seeing thatyou don't see me the same way I see you but hey I'm me and I should habve learned to accept that buy= now....but whatever...I'm not apologizing I'm not saying sorry as i saidf I wouldn't because I'm not but I wannna talk to you cause I think I need a good nights sleep sometime this fuckin millenium and I just wanted to spenmd time with youto see that you feel the same way about me that I feel about you...but I don't see that panning out...so get ahold of me, please......

↔

The dual faces of an angel come into form on the side of a broken glass. They start out as twirling shadows—blinking hypnagogic eyes—then transform into a quasi-micro galaxy. Each star in this galaxy is a shattered emotion. The stars coalesce into a distorted face. The face slowly becomes a woman. Her synapses are constantly misfiring, which causes her three eyes to blink at random. Her face is as cracked as a sun-scorched desert. Her cheeks and forehead crack open whenever she tries to smile and reveals the atrophied muscles that hide beneath her skin. She is tired and disoriented. Her equilibrium was shattered upon her transformation, which causes uncontrollably violent shaking. She is temporarily mute. A rancid green liquid flows from her mouth whenever she tries to speak. It smells like decades old vomit. She scoops it up in her cupped hands and swallos it back down. She reminds me of someone but I can't quite figure out whom. Paragraph breaks are usually assigned arbitrarily for the sake of the readers, but play hell on this author tonight. She vomits again. This time it splatters against my leg. I lap some up with my finger and taste it. It tastes like pussy. She drops down on all fours and begins to bark like a dog. Shit explodes from her rotting anus and drips onto her bruised legs. She barks and retches. Dry heaves. Gasps. Moans. She speaks—"Your realization—7 p.m. on the dawn of midnight"—I laugh. She smiles. Her face cracks. Atrophied muscles. Hell on her three eyes. Quasi-micro transformation. Shit drips. Bruised legs. Tastes like pussy.

↔

“Midnight. Dawn of the on. 7 p.m. Your realization.” I retch. She barks. Face vaguely familiar. Dual angel. I think she’s a former lover distorted by memory. I laugh. “So this is what you’ve become?” She reaches out to me. I slap her hand away. Face cracks. I fuck her dry, bloodless wound. Her pores secrete my semen. I laugh. Former memory. Atrophied lover. “So this is what you’ve become”

III.

The Last Supper

& other poems

1998-2001

An Introductory Course on Verbatimism

Verbatimism

The words flow from hyper realistic
Permutations with carved scars on
Their faces—symbolizing
The benign fears of
Monotonous strangers

A Poet creates works not with
Words but actions
Words will always come second
To his blatant desire to erase the
Sunrise

Phantasmagoria

A shattered panoramic picture of
A slaughtered vision
In which chaos tastes like honeydew
& madness washes away the soapy
Residue of your tired existence
All forms of anarchy & suppression
Are reborn in the wake of your
Mental explosion
Its tremors crucify those who ride
The present on a dead train

The formlessness of form is

Washed away with the diluted blood of
Former saviors

Throw your visions into the
Earth's Bowels and savor the moment
They're shat upon

Everything you've ever thought
Lacks the essential nutrition
Required to nourish the rose
Growing in your forehead

Dreams

Are your ally & your greatest
Betrayer
A pronunciation of their victory
Will lead to asphyxiation

No words exist

You paint new ones with your
Brush every time you set it
To paper
Kill your idols & drink their
Blood
This is a taste of
Verbatimism

New Symbols

Soluble Fish
The wound conspires
To anoint a Messiah
On the blessed fields
Of destruction

Whose constant silence
Justifies the blatant logic
Of the void

In Defense Of Chaos

An eggshell made of feathers slowly
Aborts a spiritual enigma whose elliptical
Eyes condemn the hands that feed it

As I remain perched on the ring of
A halo admiring the absence of my
Reflection in its trim

Leave Me Alone

She clutches a knife in her decayed hand
Humiliating me from the past
Her hollow eyes scream deceit
Her frozen lips indulge a cracked smile
My knees clatter as I cum in
Her mouth
She spits me into an
Ashtray and sheaths her knife
I cum and revolt
Against her plastic reflection
Her name is a cold sore upon my lip—A
Hideous infection that others see
When I speak of her demise

The Empty Bathroom

a porcelain tub filled with rust and
a placard advertising free sex sits
below a cracked roof—above a warped
floor—between a series of Orwellian
pipes—as I clean the faded
reflection of a dead lover from the
tarnished chrome of the nozzle

On Sex & Love

A twisted contortion cracks my spine
And sucks tears from my eyes
Her coarse hair scrapes my palm
As juices stain my flesh

This physical torture punctuates
A shooting pain in my head
I exile pleasure and explore her
Distant eyes while her pupils

Dilate and absorb the essence of
My misery and our passion is
Usurped by the soft spongy meats
Of distrust

Infatuation

Let's move to the South of France, shall we
And turn the black and white photos of green
Fields into a golden reality

Or shall we transfer to a quiet pond
And explore our reflections—toss in
A stone and see if my face ripples

If your nipples pop out of your loose
Fitting shirt I'll cup them with my
Hands to save you from embarrassment

We'll explore the shadows and discover
The meaning of the haunting eyes
And hollow footsteps that stalk us

As long as you swear that the blood
On your hands is from a slain beast that
Breathed its last sigh in despair

A revised discourse on

Sexuality

An ephemeral woman prevents your lidless eye from blinking

She dances in the whorls on your fingertips

& drowns your essence in a wet cough

She tickles the back of your throat with her distorted clitoris

You chew it & laugh as she feigns exhaustion

She pinches your testicles in a vice & tightens it till you're ready to explode

You rip off her nipple with your filed teeth

She removes a chunk of flesh from your neck & exchanges it for her stale gum

That's rotting in your mouth

You force your fist inside her sandy fallopian tube and open your hand

Her vibrations shatter glass frozen in a nearby windowpane

She slices the head of you penis w/ a razor

The purpose of this holy act is to mix your blood with your semen &

Denounce the crippled remnants of your essence

Realizations

My eyeballs just breathed
I felt the pupils close and
Open again
They were stunned by the
Inadequacies of the brain
Connecting their images
To thought

Tomorrow Gave Me A Headache

Tomorrow gave me a headache
This morning when I smelled the
Bitter aroma accompanying despair

A child grew before my eyes
Though I honestly doubt he's even
Been born

A collage of the sea collapsing
Played on my bedroom
Wall as I feigned sleep

I came inside a woman
I haven't met and received
A splitting headache from the future

Female Protagonist
(Juxtaposition)

A scorpion in a ring of
Fire
Panics and slaps its
Neck with its
Poisonous tail
I walk down the street
& try to
Shake the
Lit matches out of the
Hands of
Confused Christian mongers

It scurries in angles
Trying to find a way out
But the cackling child
Kneels down & laughs
As his exotic pet
Chokes on its own
Bile
They gather around me
& prohibit me from moving
As their miserable God
Kneels down beside us
& readies
Himself for the show

Playboy

A hand cups a firm
Breast reflecting the light of my eyes
It warms the life sustaining milk
As its nipple flutters like a flower in winter

Rolling down an inch or two where the
Dark pink shadows reveal a soft
Outline of ribs collapsing into
A frozen stomach

Traveling up again to the right
Breast—fully exposed—
Without a gentle hand to conceal it—
The soft pink nipple is profiled

I can taste milk
Trickling from the breast
Torn from a magazine and know
That her essence has prolonged my life

Though her chest and torso remain
Intact the rest of her body is missing
But that doesn't stop me from seeing
My face in her eyes

nine-eleven

It's raining dust and soot
Inside a posh upper class
Dining room

Glass and body parts
Fall from the sky

As a screaming Eagle
Disappears into its own fiery
Reflection

What scares me more than
The initial explosion is
Cleaning up the broken pieces

The Waking Dead Are
Bored & Misplaced

Cemeteries—
Memories chiseled
In stone
Cancerous palms
Silently trace
The blue hues
At dawn
Wondering who
Made them

#41

An ounce of
Tears
    Are worth
    A
Brick of
    Gold
When sorrow
Reigns
And your
Eyes bleed
      Dust

10 Fragments For *Her*

1. It amazes me that the sun
Still hangs around your
Neck and that the moon continues
To dance in your eyes

2. I'd rather gnaw on a tablet
Of cyanide than to hear
Another cock falling out
    Of your jaded mouth

3. O'! How you piss me off with
Those morning eyes
    That paper frown and
    Those lithe fingers
    Dancing on the tip of
    My cigarette

4. Sometimes I push my thumbs
Into my eyes and try to erase your
Portrait from the back of
    My eyelids
    But it never works
And I'm forced to examine the
Curvature of your face at
Three in the morning

5. I don't understand why you're
Still here
With me
Alone
At four in the morning as
I concede to the fact that
Worlds will never spring from
These fingertips

6. I can't stomach the thought
Of looking into your eyes
And seeing another man's
Reflection

7. Will you fucking choose either
The Sun or the Moon
Because I need one to fucking
See

8. Allow me to apologize for
Waking the heavens but
Powerful tremors rock my body
Because the stars refuse
Me

9. Your soul leaps out
And burns every nerve in
My body

10. Give me a night to drape
My arm over your shoulders
To soil your ribs with my

Fingers

    To taste your lips and to

    See my smile in your eyes

And I'll bless you with all of

    God's golden heaven—

Then I'll happily recede into

The darkness and return you to

Yourself

The birth of a Verbatimist

Void
A supersonic hyper-frequency rattles the
Scattered canyons like a blast inside a
Shotgun barrel

Nothingness
Darkness opens & expands the
First taste of
Movement

His gelatinous fingers open & close
Open & close
Open & close
Until he grasps the understanding
Of sensation
Or so he thinks—sensation is an insect
That can be caught or a crow that one
Can perch on his scarred shoulder

So he wafts the sands of eternity with
His hard rubber hands
& curses the spirits for spitting it back
In his face

His serpentine gestures attracts
Only the quaintest of foes
While his sensitive predisposition
Repels the infidels who lack
A fear of desire

He curses his antecedents & rushes
Out to the local butcher shop &
Requests the removal of a faulty
Portion of his brain

They refuse him so he assaults them
With fists full of feces & cripples
Their ignorance with a blow from his
Mighty quill

This is the beginning of his tortured
Fable
All roads lead to nowhere which is
Exactly where he intends to be

So he dances on the fault
Lines on the edge of town
Curses the night with his
Impassioned fruits
& bids farewell to those who
Never got to know him

He waits for a thought to
Wisk him away & laughs at
The martyrs dancing in the
Clouds

If only they knew what it meant
To be insincere

Que Sera—says he—
Till we meet again my loves

He discards his thoughts &
Wanders down the road
Just as a vision
Pulls into the abandoned
Freight yard

Chaos Theory

an ivory arrow slashes
a white shroud like a
hypnagogic speck reintroducing
you to the fragrance of movement

the freak blizzard dancing
in its wake coalesces with my
arched spine

immaculate eyes wander the void and
shower the horizons with bitter
thoughts

as light retracts into the belly
of the sun and I'm left with
darkness shining on my
brow

wondering whatever happened to
the butterfly in the
park

Song

The wings of a feather
Crack like a dove
In autumn
When the rain subsides
And shadows lurk
In the darkest recesses
Of your mind

Poem

I strike a match and
gently remove a tick
from my cat's ear as
her jewish thoughts
hang on Hitler

Picking dead skin
from my index finger
I watch it
transform into a
moth and fly through
the sealed window

Sometimes I contemplate
Rimbaud's salvation in
the desert and wonder if
I'm doing the right thing

A Pun

(for Rimbaud)

O' Arthur!
Did Verlaine teach
    you that all
    assholes are
different
when he shot you
    in that grimy
    Brussels hotel
    room?

In praise of chaos

Laughing we sing & shuffle
A thousand ants into a shotgun
Barrel
We dance on walls & speak
In confused acrylics
A gelatinous child grows outside
A beast's vulgar belly
We laugh & poke it as we
Chart its progress
The terrorist country &
Cocky community facilitates
Our desire to dance in the
Eye of the storm
A metallic flower collapses
Upward & disappears into the
Soggy heavens
Its brother collapses with
Exhaustion
We defy the cowardly
Suggestions of silencing
Our inhibitions in times
Such as these
All men are free of thought
Except for those who want
It
So we carry on & pretend
This will not be our last
Dance together
Laughing we sing & shuffle
A thousand ants into a shotgun
Barrel
We dance on walls & speak
In confused acrylics

Angels & Devils

I dream of Angels
Every now & then

Sometimes they reap whirlwinds
At other times they are prudent &
Suggestive

Their indignant wings
Cut me when they brush
Against
Me

I cry
Lord how I cry

I watch their eyeballs
Roll out of their heads
& stop in the middle of
The room

They suddenly expand &
This microcosmic tear
Introduces me to a new
World—

One where Angels
Admire my sense of
Destruction—
I dream of Devils
Every now & then

Sometimes they are sublime
In their absurdity
At other times they cower
Beneath my thoughtful gaze

They give birth to the
Madness locked behind
My eyes

I cry
Lord how I cry

Awake, Dreaming

I wake and give mercy to my love   I stare into her heart & hear the cool tears slide down her cheeks as I pretend to look away

O'! What mysteries hide

behind her cool calm eyes

She embraces a vat of fire & retires in a brutal pyre

Sometimes I wake just to touch her thigh & breathe a sigh as I see the sky in her folded eyes

Her warm breath splatters against my neck like a forgotten kiss

I don't

think she knows where she wants to be   surely it isn't here   it's not beside me

But

what can I do as I lay here & wonder if tomorrow will come & I'll be undone by the flickering sun   as   it attempts to wake me by breaking up the black pigments of my stapled curtains

So I'll shun it away

Until the day

That I can rise and clearly say

"Life, O' Love, to you I give everything & in return I ask for nothing"

But right now that day isn't here so I'll shun the present, ignore the past, and take up residence in the future

As I stare into my love's heart & dream of the mysteries

locked

Behind her cool calm folded eyes

Her warm breath splatters against my neck

like a forgotten kiss

I don't
think she knows where she wants to be   surely it isn't here   it's not beside me

A Poem

for Clara Bow

Your mad eyes trace the evolution of the
Feminist movement back to the days when your
Mother tried to kill you

Your tired hands—now rotting—reminds
Me of the soft velvet touch of my grandmother
I only make this connection, I suppose, because
You're of the same ilk

Your soft, milky stomach makes me shudder
At the thought of slipping my tongue into your
Once youthful & admirable cunt

Your mad feet dance when music is no longer
There—your face distrusts the farcical receptions
Of this maddening, insane life what awful
Things did it to you as a kid

O' Clara! Where have you gone? Where has
It gone? Can you still cry on demand? Was all
The bullshit you went through worth it?

You ended up no better off than your mother
Crazy, insane, isolated, afraid to come to terms
With the thoughts in your head

So you ran from them—you…you! Who never
Ran from anything—and locked yourself inside
The heart of the desert only to wither
Like a malnourished flower

O' Clara! Dear, sweet Clara! Whose eyes stare
At me from the past, whose hips dance in peristaltic
Glory, whose smile cuts through my heart

You look so sad now, as you stare off the page
In your manly tie & suspenders—only you, Clara,
Only you could steal my heart, now

I think about the time I dreamt of you &
Bettie Page   we were on a safari—or a
Satori, I can't remember which—and you
Left early so you could inspire someone else

& I was left with Bettie, who did nothing
For me because I'd already met you—and, like
Every other woman I've ever met—

I was obsessed with you and you wanted
Nothing to do with me, so I hung out with
Bettie who'd stolen my heart as a child

But I longed for you, dear Clara, for your
Heart, your soul, your powerfully decadent
Spirit, your freedom, your madness, &
What is madness but complete freedom?

So I prayed that you'd return   night after
Night I slept for days, never leaving my bed,
Hoping that you'd come to me

I felt like a leper   I waited for you in the
Back of Adam's car   I waited for you while
I got drunk in the solemn night

O' Clara! I waited for you to come to me
But the problem was—as I see it now—that I
Saw you looking at me through someone
Else's eyes and, like you, she rejected me

So I gave up, my love, I'm sorry   I gave
  Everything away and regressed back to my
Miserable youth   now I am back

  And I no longer wait for you, sweet
Clara, because you are dead &
  I must move on

Our Last Trip

Do you remember
The day the
Earth died? We
Took a ride
To taste the wind
One last time
To bid the night
A fond farewell
Do you remember
The sun's visage?
Watching her final
Descent from the
Promenade?
Do you remember
The rabid cheers?
Applause?
Young couples
Bathing in her
Last light?
Do you remember?

The Forgotten Poet

His drunken eyeballs
Floated in his sunken
Face like lily
Pads
In grimy waters
Painting the canvas
Purchased at nature's
Expense—only
To find the paintings
Dissolved

Lamenting Desire

"Fuck you," said the hand to
the face as its fingers
peeled his eyes from their
rotting sockets

"No, fuck you," retorted the
distorted face as his
mouth intervened and hastily
bit off his fingers

"What did you say?" Asked the
twin hand wielding jagged
knife and proceeded to cut out
his eyes

"You don't need anybody," said
his heart, pumping
diseased blood into his tired
body forcing face and hands to rest

The Lion's Tail

Oh no I've done it now

The sun sets in the east and

Grows in the west

A curious lion shaking his

Tail provoked the clouds

A city is founded in the

Future and annihilates

The past

Its citizens neglect the

Present

Fire and snakes circle its

Buildings—in a swirl of

Activity—as they race

To the heavens

Minarets stifle their

Laughter as they pretend to

Be inanimate

Poets and visionaries engage

In endless activity

As they gather 'round to

Commemorate the collapse

Of the bureaucratic

Empire

Children lacerate

Themselves and

Watch their blood dance

Down their arms and

Dive into the earth's

Green hands

The sun sweeps across

The sky—drowning ghosts

In pools of light

Provoked by the lion's tail

The clouds grow in numbers

Preventing the sun from

Flooding my face

And that beautiful city

Recedes

Until it is only a

Memory

Poem

I wipe the
  Amphetamine
From your
Cheek and follow
  The trails back
Up to your sorrowful
Eyes—your breath is
  The only drug
That gets me high
In your eyes I see
The future where
You allow me to give
  Children your eyes
And my smile—in them
I see a warm home
  Where death is not
Allowed—only love
In them I see a woman
Who can love me for
Who I am not what I
Appear to be
  And I lick my moist
Fingers I die—O'! how I
Die!

Fuck You Illuminated

Forgotten Men
Unknown to the world
Can't deny their
Killer's instinct

You were stuck in
Oceans of blood
Utterly alone

Lonely Night

The Sun and Moon leave saliva
Tracks on my forearm. My loin
Thrusts against the wind as
Raindrops burn my torso

The howling wind is obscured by
The sound of flesh eating flesh. My
Eyeballs float through the

Clouds as they search for a
Universe in which to place the
Stars hanging from my fingertips

I turn and stare at the
Whispering trees beneath an empty
Sky and sleep in a puddle of stars
wasted on a lonely night

The Disillusionment

Of Intimacy

A nipple converges with a
Breath of air

And is taken seriously
Until a drop of

Milk blinds a
Toothless eye

And discredits its
Spiritual nature

Offerings To A Muse

I offer the meat of this world
In a bowl bound by flesh and the
Splintered fragments of a
Useless skull

I offer the eyes of my dear
Mother, as interpreted by my
Father's undying lust

I offer the purity of a cock
That hasn't been exposed to
The milky eye of conception

I offer the mist of an ethereal
Companion, cloaked in a veil of
Tears, to you my liege

In exchange for a glimpse into
The void that once eclipsed
Man's mortal eyes

An Open Invitation To 'Poets' & 'Visionaries'

A legacy of fire is only as good
As the pyre on which it was laid
To those who speak in tangled
Tongues & confuse even themselves
In an attempt to open the
Heavens

I give to you this
Dagger
On which countless poems have
Been displayed
& offer the option to solidify
Your art with a modicum
Of dignity & truth

Genesis

A single sperm copulates with a breath of
   Air inside a forlorn sand blown seashell
A swift tide carries the breathless lamentation
To the sea where it sinks and gives birth to
   A rising tsunami
That gathers momentum & collapses upon
A shore where angels have staked their
Claim
Their silent wings are stifled
They repress their faith & move out into
   The streets where anarchy is born
In the heart of children watching God
Being given to the masses
The children revolt & denounce the
Message brought forth by the liberated
Angels   they are abruptly slaughtered
      No peace in the eyes of God
Shouts the neo-anarchists who rose
From the ashes of their fathers
      Everything means nothing
      When nothing means everything
      & We devote ourselves to stories
      Relegated to neurotics & sadists
Rise up against those who claim to know
You & send them to heaven w/ god lumped
In their throats

She Haunts Me

She haunts me
    She haunts me tho' I don't know her
She haunts me
In my sleep
In my eyes when they drift heavenward
In my soul when I long for forgiveness
In my ears when I remember her breath
In my tongue whose molecules longed to
    Expand & taste her
In my thoughts where she continues to haunt me
In my imagination where I pretended she wasn't
    Really there
In my heart where I didn't know she roamed
In my past for facilitating my ignorance
She haunts me
    She haunts me tho' I don't know her
She haunts me
In my bed where I finger the fading remnants
    Of her indentation

Wet Dreams

Madness
The void disintegrates
In the palm of
My hand
As starry-eyed
Angels
Fade into
The cool remnants
Of a jaded
Moon

The Secret

Did you know the eyes you
  Look through—the elongated iris
That takes a deep breath & exhales
A simple tear or two—
          Did you know your sweet lips
That slightly tightens
          That kisses the intangible
          Petals of my breath
That parts in a tiny o
          As you fight
                  To understand the
                  Feelings w/in
Did you know your
                  Smooth hair
     That   Kisses sweetly
                  My coarse
                  Flesh
                         Did you know your
                  Gentle hand
                         That dances
                         W/ the nicotine
                         Stained ozone
Inches away
                 From my
                       Hand
     Did you know your sweet breath
                 That entices me so
That makes me shudder
            As it breaks
                 Apart my
                 Broken skin
  Suffocates me
  W/an air of
            Neglect &
                    Despair

A Brief Conversation

ME: I don't know the world

YOU: I keep telling you we're
Just passing through

ME: I don't know
The sun

YOU: I keep telling you it's
Just passing
Through

ME: I don't know
My
Soul

YOU: I keep telling you
It's
Just passing through

ME: I don't know
You

YOU: I
Keep telling
You
I'm just
Passing through

Key To Enlightenment

Two creatures walk down a broken
Street carrying the same set of eyes
They move past a decaying house
Where the remnants of a child's laughter

Haunts her suicidal father. In the
Shadows cast by an angelic statue, a
Disenchanted boy injects his juices into
The rotting anus of a dead dog.

The creatures watch this with mute
Curiosity and move on as they predict that
A large crowd will gather up the street.
They make their way through the cramped

Flesh and are overjoyed to see people
Picking dead flesh from a rotting cadaver
Perched atop a splintered
Cross. They withdraw a rusty knife and

Remove a large chunk of meat from the
Savior's thigh. They swallow his
Essence, drinking his juices with stilted
Chagrin. A meandering child takes a peak

Beneath the cloth 'round the Savior's waist
And runs away with disappointment etched
On her young face. The creatures feel a
Burning sensation in the pit of their

Stomachs and drop to their knees, retching,
Trying to purge themselves of the unholy
Decadence. After emancipating their stomachs
Of the original sin, they move beyond the

Crowd as a sadistic heretic approaches the
Cross with a smile on his face. They take a
Final disdainful look at the suffering liar
And laugh at the crowd that has sacrificed

Logic to be by his side. They watch
With mute curiosity as a disenchanted
Young man injects his juices into the rotting
Anus of the dead man. They laugh and move

On as they predict that a large crowd will
Gather 'round a shiny brick of gold up the
Street, where they continue to search for
The key to enlightenment.

A Renunciation

Of Beauty

I woke and looked outside
In time to see a
Great burst of energy fill
The air

Clouds dispersed; rooftops
Collapsed. The concussion from
The psychic wave
Rippled the concrete.

A cacophony of moans filled
The air like a roaring thunder.
Restless townsfolk poured
Into the streets and watched

A wave of fire paint
The sky. They braced themselves
For their first sunrise; they
Panicked.

—How can such beauty exist
Without having been projected
Through my television? Asked a
Man whose retinas have been

Scarred by Hollywood. —This
Can't be, said a virgin who was
Tricked into celibacy by Jesus
Christ himself.

—She's right, proclaimed someone
Else. This is all an illusion. He
Points to the sun as it makes
A perfect arc across the

Sky and assures them
That nothing this powerful could
Exist in the real world. They
Agree and remove their eyes,

Moving toward their houses,
Their lies. And the
Power of the sun is diminished
By the blue hues of television

At dawn. And that burst
Of energy that shook me from my
Bed recedes until it is but
An afterthought.

Emily Illuminated

E is for the
beauty dancing
over the horizon

M recalls the
sun dipping in
the ocean

I is for the
person continuing
to haunt me

L is for the
emotions swimming to
the surface

Y recalls the
sorrow of having
let you go

1st Manifesto

A symmetrical landscape born in
The throat dies in the
Ear
Flaccid demons float on lily pads
In silver streams that are
Broken down into putrefied
Syllables
The brilliance of a sparrow's
Assault on a tree's flesh is
Interpreted as a
Verb phrase
Shoddy syntax discredits
The beautiful description of
A soul blighted by
Morality
A modern Queen resting in
The palm of a muscle is
Obscured by
Antiquity
Words shall be seduced by
Sensitive flesh and deemed
Archaic by the crumpled
Podiums of a fallen
Empire

2nd Manifesto

A person's life work is reflected
In a pinprick of blood. In
This microcosm lays a vast library
As great as a thousand points of
Light.
Each book in this genealogical
Marketplace is bound with the
Preserved flesh of repressed
Memories.
The right pen treats this
Droplet as an immaculate
Tool conceived to exhume the
Memories resting
Within the honeycomb tiers of
The divine ink. Only then
Will the story of past sunsets
Remind us of a time we can't
Recall.

Footnote To Manifestoes

I sit beneath a frozen stream
Resting my arm on
The shore

Words ripple through the
Imagined waters and posses
My feeble mind

I try to escape the diminishing
Tide, but the syllabic waves
Grow larger

In a desperate attempt to swim
To the horizon, I alienate
The only land I know

And find myself stranded in the
Center of a shimmering maelstrom
Of thought

Song

Curse in a void
I attempt to
Hear
Simple thoughts
In complex
Air
Creating for you
A soul and a
Lie
From splintered
Remnants of
Reality

Winter Solstice

A man dances with a water
Hose, sharing his emotions
With the wet lawn

A child mends the wounds
on his bicycle with
the sunset dancing in his
eyes

a massive serpent writhes
in the background, each
scale a leaf mosaic

countless cars swim through
the streets, their occupant
sharing a single vision,
uniting them with the
boy, the serpent, and the man

If You Could See How I Feel:

My flesh boils with
Lesions
It cracks and turns
To dust
But not before
Its colors change
To black coal
My organs
Harden and fill
With a bile as dark
As night and as
Thick as concrete
My brain swells
Then shrinks
As my lungs
Collapse and flake
Away
But I'm still
Alive
As muscles atrophy
I'm still
Alive
As my stomach
Hungers for your
Nutrients
I'm still
Alive
But not for long

Soon your crashing
Wave will recede
Into the
Ocean from which
You sprang
And I'll be nothing
More than a pile
Of sand

4 Interpretations Of

Popular Dali Motifs

1.

A rock dances on your forehead
Shaped by the feet of your
Ancestors three hundred years before
The consecration of the jelly in your eyes

2.

A lion dances around your inert body as
You fight to fuck and pretend to ignore
A fiery woman dancing at your fingertips
She is not aware of the depths of your soul

3.

Your cock has been formed into cold steel and
Placed on a black hilt in the hands of a
Woman who plunges it into her moist cunt
Because you left heaven without the need to kill

4.

A swarm of ants scurry up your virgin body
And attempt to carry you to heaven only
To be squashed by a promiscuous grasshopper
Ejaculating into your trembling mouth

Delayed Reaction

Your words may take a thousand
years to roll off your tongue
but I hear them at last
and they resonate with the energy
of an earthquake at dawn

they split my skin
and my flesh flakes
like burnt sand
my desert is desolate
and you're the wanderer who refuses
to enter my bleak realm

and my fragile grains rot away

I'm empty and alone
and know that your flesh will
never caress my body so I must avoid
the hurt and wish you the best
and say goodbye although I can't do
it goodbye may your fertile
soil enlighten another while
I rot away goodbye

Song

Your soul is my
Wine
How I'd love to
Dine
On the light you
Divine

Rebirth

Planting is the
Seed of self
Blooming are the
Thorns of
Sacrifice
And the gentle
Rose
Whose flesh is
Covered with
Blood
Moves toward
The
Benevolent
Heavens
Breaking the
Skin of
The fertile
Sun

The Broken Angel

An angel is carried across a
Sea of mud by wings made of tears
Streams of sand flow from the
Wound concealing her heart
She stares into the eye of
The hurricane, looking for a mind
Eager to mend her broken thoughts
Moving away from the pain
That haunts her she takes
Refuge in a land populated by
Lonely demons
The promiscuous monsters
Laugh as they prod her wound
With a thousand fiery tongues
They invite her to join them
Inside the brooding cunt of
An indifferent God
She protests, the God she's
Searching for must have a warm
Hand and a friendly smile
And she refuses to tread over
Immaculate water until she
Meets a receptive God who will
Give her everything

The Ballad of

Zabibah & the King

All the sheep & lemmings crowded together in a coward's
Room
They clutched their sweaty papers and silently read
To themselves
A denunciation of evil, they exclaimed
Renounce the villainous bearcats & serpents
Who so desire to perpetrate violence on an innocent
Culture
Little do they know that this innocent culture hides behind
A violent Queen who once murdered her own screaming children
& a million lambs who couldn't smell their own fate until
It was too late
This Queen rests perched on a tarnished throne
Even with her eyes plucked out she would sell her
Kingdom as long as she remained on the throne

Cool thoughtless air streaks through the dirt
Streets & oil fields
It is without odor & form
Its real form takes place in the bloodless eye
It explodes through bleeding pores
Hardens the lungs
And atrophies the kidney
Taking on the shape of death herself

A weeping child stands with her arms
Crossed at her chest
Her hands resting on her shoulders

She tries to look angelic but she can
Feel the Queen looking down on her
A blind man's portrait of the Queen
Dances on the wall behind her &
Keeps a fascistic eye on all of her
Children
They are well trained to the notion of
Being eaten by their smiling mother

The Queen takes a Baath
In the ignorance of youth
Those wide-eyed pupils
Who were frightened by the
Glowing monarchy
But their inability to move
Forward plunged them into
A brick shower
& the Queen remained there
For five years
Dreaming of Sajida
& the five crystals uniting
Their third eye

After the shower
She crawled up the light posts
Past the faded posters denouncing
A revolution
Soon She hid behind the flaking
Façade of a demon known as
Bakr

When Bakr collapsed

He bequeathed the throne to
Our Queen
Whom we so adore &
Defend
Her first rule of order was
The execution of her rivals

There she languished
On an ever fading
Throne
Her people were nothing more
Than gristle that She separated
From the meat & partitioned
On the vacant side of the
Plate

Then She slaughtered the
Lambs
Who didn't like her feast & vowed
To feed their brethren food
Of a different ilk
They paid the ultimate price
For their vision
She raised fear by
Razing towns and drowning
Wetlands with a new form of
Madness

Yet at the same time she erected vast statues depicting
Her kindness
She wore the silk hat of benevolence & a warm smile
She commissioned towering portraits of herself to

Be hung on crumbling walls
These portraits paint pictures of a good Queen
A noble Queen who cares about her children
They do not show the reality of her children running
Away in fear of being eaten

Our Queen was made to look like Hemingway
In these silent portraits

She rose up and surprised her neighbors who were far
Stronger than she had predicted
They squashed her minions & drove her into a form of
Depression
She didn't lament the deaths of hundreds of thousands
Of children
Only the fact that her throne had been tarnished

Later she tried to secure water for her machines from
A neighbor who didn't want to lower its price
Her resentment swallowed her better half
& she sent her children into the desert
With guns blazing & voices raised

This proved to be her undoing

The serpent famous for gnawing on its
Tail from time to time
Slithers into the desert   leaving stress
Marks on the sand
The Queen remains steadfast
She gave her son who fell from her
Bruised vagina a present that sent tremors

Through the many worlds that strive to survive
In the countless grains of sand
These Revolutionary Guards
Are sure to squash the serpent before
It rises up & sprays them with its
Venom

The Queen proclaims this to be a shining moment
In the history of her world
She will survive the mother of all wars
As a child reborn into the madness
Of the night

But her vanity proves stronger than her
Own reflection & the serpent injects its juices
Into her back

She triumphs as she is eaten alive

Her children pray for the poisons to
Kick in but she proves stronger than she appears
To be

She lays in one of her secret beds
Nestled away inside the shiny golden walls
Of one of her many hidden palaces
She reads the history of her people
& must know that she will fall like all of the
Kings & Queens who came before her

But her delusions persist

She envisions a world united by her wisdom
A world whose children worship her with a
Rabid tenacity
But her vision is spoiled by the reality of her actions
For her children will rise up & squash her eventually
Even when the serpent's venom takes its toll on her
She will bequeath her throne to an unjust heir
He will follow in her footsteps & silence the children
With gaseous fear
But the children will be exhausted & tired of running
From a single entity
They will revolt & take out all of their hatred for
The Queen on the poor foolish tyrant who replaced
Her
& the legacy that she dreams up
As she lays in her secret bed
Will slip into a forgotten corner of the desert
& will be buried by a wind reminding
Her of an entire nation's hatred for her

But until that day comes she will continue
To slaughter her children on the blessed
Blood fields of her ego

Until the day the Serpent persists
And drives the wicked Queen from her home
Before she is afforded the opportunity to pass
Her wrath onto a disciple
Then the Serpent proves itself fair &
Gnaws on its tail once again

& You

You lambs you lemmings defend her
You lambs & lemmings who crowd together in a crowded room
Clutching your sweaty papers & silently awaiting your
Chance to denounce
The flawed serpent
Who occasionally gnaws on its
Own tail
For attacking the poor defenseless vicious Queen &
Silencing her before she has a hand in squashing the serpent
You poor lambs You poor lemmings
You who defend her
Poor lambs Poor lemmings
Poor lambs Poor lemmings
Fuck you lambs Fuck you lemmings
Rot in this coward's room while I reenter the real
World
Free of conscience

Transmutation

I.

A boy stands alone in
A forest
  Knee deep in
Mud
His loneliness has
Sealed his mind's eye
His vision uproots
   Him
And plants him in a
Garden
Where waves
Silently lick
The calm Earth

II.

He moves with

Peristaltic grandeur
Investigating this
Strange new
World
Unable to believe
He hasn't left
His room
Unable to comprehend
The power of
His dreams

III.

A snake surreptitiously
Writes in the
                    Sand
Wrapping its cold flesh
Around nature's
                    Third eye
As it disdainfully shuns
The boy's powerful
                    Imagination

IV.

And in a sudden moment
Of transmutation
                    An
Ephemeral bolt of
                    Lightening
Is bound for heaven
Leaving shards of coarse
                    Glass in its
Wake

The Last Supper

I.

I was born
Twenty years
Ago

Not a hundred
Or a
Thousand
But twenty

Although I
Have many
Selves

I have never
Been anybody
Else

I have seen
The haunting
Reality of
The human
Psyche

The warped
Shadows
Turn
Into flesh

I have seen
Children cower
In
Darkness

Obsessively
Searching their
Bodies for
Gaping
Wounds

Who've
Anticipated
The great
Deluge

Nuclear fallout
And the invasion
Of foreign
Troops

I have seen
Callow young
Boys
Contemplating
Inconceivable
Notions
Analyzing
Situations
They would never
Understand till
They've experienced

Themselves

What they
Think they
Know

I have seen
Young writers
Cultivate madness
As an
Alternative to
Experience

Alchemists who
Weave
Myriad-eyed
Demons into
Weak prose

Teenagers who
Have abused
Alcohol and
Narcotics out
Of boredom

Children who've
Longed for
Internal
Experience

And denounced
The external
World

Fifteen year
Olds burnt out
Hooked on
Cigarettes
Alcohol
Marijuana
Bent on
Escaping the
Inescapable and
Pronouncing the
Ineffable

I have seen
Torment
And dementia
Induced by
Drugs tobacco
And sleep
Deprivation

Terrifying
Outbursts that
Could not be
Contained

I have seen a
Thousand new
Beginnings

Lost young men
Escaping the
Hand that holds
Them down

Drifting over
Dark horizons
Walking on broken
Glass

Reflecting
Broken images of
The sun

Nursing addiction
With borrowed
Sweat

Meeting a
Virgin daughter
Who saw his
Soul every time
She looked in
The mirror

Their
Relationship
Was a fruitful
One

They cultivated
Dreams and
Developed a new
Form of
Literature

But union
Manifests
Insanity and
They began
To abuse one
Another

Drinking blood
From fresh
Wounds

Indulging in
Sex as a means
Of
Alienation

Giving glass
Tattoos

Sleeping on
Blood stained
Sheets and
Inevitably
Parting ways

Enacting
Tragedies that
Once fueled
Their
Imaginations

Kindred souls
Embrace one
Another
Until they
Rot away

II.

Curious young
Men search the
Night
Looking for
Answers

Dreaming on
The wet lawn
Smoking
Cigarettes and
Planning their
Destruction

Vodka floats
In their
Stomachs

As they
Masturbate
In the
Dark

And sacrifice
Their children
To the milky
Moon

What time
They've wasted
On flesh
What woman
Would allow such
A vile creature
To violate her

Their eyes
Weave prisms
Of light

While caressing
A woman's curves
With their
Mind's eye

And they sleep
In empty beds
Accepting their
Loneliness and
Longing for death

But emptiness and
Loneliness drive
Their obsession
To create new
Worlds and
Languages

Alone
They fabricate
Women and harvest
Delusions such
As acquiring
Women through
Literature

Women want
Neither writers nor
Intellectuals

They want a
Mantle piece
A silent
Superficial
Troglodyte
With a big
Dick and an
Equally
Impressive
Wallet

I have seen
Men fall apart
Upon realizing
They'll
Never attain
Beauty

And beauty alone
Attracts
Beauty

Not the
Philosophical
Indictments of a
Naïve monster

And in response
To their awakening
They become rabid
Beasts

Who dive into
Glass oceans
Shattering the
Arrows of the sun
With the
Remnants of a
Wave

And wander the
Streets
Looking for

Lost women
Who specialize
In emotions

Sharing
Bosch's vision
Of flying fish
Crooked priests
And meat houses
With a door
Parting the anus

Who laugh at
Their
Contemporaries

And look for
The eyeballs
Lurking in
The sky

Hiding behind
Heavenly
Sky-lids

They sit in
A daze
Watching
History unfold
On their
Window

As the walls
Around them
Pulse and
Sweat blood
Watching in
Astonishment as
The blood
Drips upward
Until the ceiling
Is covered with
A million red
Domes

And when
Vision becomes
Reality

Life itself is
An
Hallucinogenic
World

And they spend
Their nights
Hiding
Within the
Sacred halls
Of their
Decadent
Sanctuaries

Flesh junkies
Wander the
Streets looking
For a
Fix
Bent on death
Destruction
And locating
Whitman's
America

Leaving the
Blood soaked
Hills of
Golgotha
Unimpressed

Repressing
Their fears
And returning
To the meat
Maelstrom

III.

I have seen
More than I
Would have
Cared to

And
Every time
I have
Revealed myself
To the
Naked
Eye
Although I
Have many
Selves
Most remain

Estranged

I am no
Longer a
Person
No longer
A poet
But an
Observer

One who
Perceives
And
Acknowledges
The events
Within

I have
Failed to retain
My identity
Countless times

The voyeur
Must remain
Incognito or
He is
Discredited
And his works
Remain
Ineffective

IV.

The Lost Book of the Dead

2003

The Lost Book of the Dead

(as transcribed by a frightened Verbatimist)

Texts relating to the
Etiology of despair

O' Osiris to thee I dictate my soul
Whose holy words & crooked scepter transforms the sands of youth
Into brittle insecure sheets of glass
Whose Ka is tarnished
Who embodies the holy trinity devoid of passion & spirituality
To thee I sacrifice the limbs of my father   the eyes of my mother &
The youthful torment that engulfs them
Your form—dear Osiris, my liege—appears to have manifested
Through the ages
I enter the blessed temple & recognize you although you appear to be
Shrouded in blasphemous delusions
I tasted your essences when I stopped in Anu to quench my thirst
For knowledge
Its tastes were unlike anything I'd ever tasted before—dear liege
I danced & stripped myself of this mortal clothing
I looked down & spied Maati
Until that very second I assumed it was either nonexistent or well
Hidden
But I glimpsed it for the briefest of moments & to you I pledge my
Undying devotion
In hopes that you will introduce me to Khepera—I've but a few
Words to share with him & I hope & pray that he'll listen
Osiris I fear *you* may not be listening to me

I give myself to you
Place me on your alter & abolish the demons hiding behind
My smile
I have visions of a Woman rushing through a blizzard with
A soul trapped in her gut
A soul trying to break through to the blissful
Realm of consciousness
Where has this come from—my dear liege—I do not recall this
Is this your work
Dear Osiris the establisher of truth
Have you planted the seeds of this vision into my milky eyes
Show me how to nourish them
I slip through the void & hover inside a black hole
Its vacuum cripples the light
Coiled snakes wrap around my right arm
I think it's my hand but I can't feel a thing
I'm burnt & choking on placenta
My nerve endings do not yet recognize the velvet softness of touch
Osiris He who gives life to Ra
Are you doing this to me
I've never experienced such peace
To what do I owe the pleasure
Oh no   I feel it coming   I'm afraid   cradle me in the warm arms
Of assurance
Osiris
Where have you gone   my liege
Streaks of light & thunderous roars blow through the darkness
Flashes of pink meat dance in the fleeting rays of light
An earthquake usurps the silence & splits the darkness at its moist
Hairy edges

Light creeps into its crevices & illuminates my fingers   they
Are translucent
I can see inside myself   nothing registers   everything is foreign
I gag on milky bile dancing in my throat   I can't take
This my liege
What are you doing to me   where have you misplaced me
A pocket of air strips the pulsating walls of its protective film
I hear distant voices   they sound almost as if they're submerged in
Water   I can't decipher the dialogue   it sounds like a crude discourse
On Epiphanies
Light grows like the ring of a supernova   blinding the
Pink shadows   I extend my weightless arms   feeling is borne in my
Thoughts   the walls feel moist & raw   bluish green veins run around in
Circles
Ra's mammoth hand emerges from the slit in the heavens & fishes around
For my head
What shall I do dear sweet Osiris
Where are you my liege   does the specter of Seth still haunt you
Do you still cower O' holy one
My head is pounding   Ra has me   what shall I do
I writhe & convulse   I'm choking   I feel my face turning blue
I slip through the void
Oh god the light   the light   I am blinded   the drowned men & women
Continue to haunt me   they laugh & applaud   their clattering bones rock
My head   I can't breathe   what shall I do my liege
I'm suddenly wrapped in the gentle cloth of adolescence   O' what a feeling
What a feeling my liege

Homage to thee dear Osiris   to what do I owe the pleasure

Everything is new   holy   mysterious   *sensual*   I touch & taste everything

Nothing scares me   although I lack the proper coordination to move I sway with

The music of laughter

Emotions take their form   I see vibrations & hear colors   everything is holy

& divine

O' how great this new world is   you really must attend its symphony sometime

Even you—my liege—would fall to your knees in tears

I have my first brush with fame   I don't mind it   I am too obsessed with my

Own mommy   I can feel myself forming in the ashes of her rejection

My daddy   whom I once resented for stealing my mommy's warmth is now

My best friend

It is he who has captured my thoughts   I model myself after him   I will not

Disappoint him

My sister has suddenly appeared   she robs me of my

Idols   I don't like her much   I try to sell her to the tall man next-door

He has bushy hair over his top lip   he frightens me with his booming voice

He laughs at me & tells mommy that I tried to sell Jamie   mommy laughs

& messes up my hair   the bushy-lipped neighbor man laughs too

I don't get it   what'd I miss

Flashes of time   where has it gone

I'm in a tube being shot through the air   brown & green plaid blankets float

Past the windows   I watch a bazillion ants dance around   their tiny cars

Look funny from up here   we land in a desert   weird green things hurt my fingers

We're all around a pool with my mommy's sisters & their babies

I can't go in   they say I'm not big enough   but I am big enough   I don't like

Watching my mommy's sister's babies having all the fun   I'll show them who's

Big enough   I jump in   splash   I fall to the bottom   my eyes burn

It hurts when I breathe   I try to cough   water comes out of my nose

My mommy is dancing around   she's crying   don't cry mommy   I try to

Go to her but I can't move   I cough   my head feels funny   my mommy &

Her sister's babies look funny from down here   they're all long & squiggly

My mommy's sister's son jumps into the pool   he swims really good he looks

Kinda like a fish   he grabs me & flies me to the top   I laugh   my throat & eyes

Burn   my mommy hugs me & cries on my shoulder   I laugh at her funny

Mommy   where's my sister   I finally get all the attention again

My first brush with death

O' Osiris   I sing to you   bring me back   my head hurts   I want to cry

Wave the crooked scepter & cure me of this acute schizophrenia

My dear sweet liege   where have you gone

Flashes of time   streaks of gray & white

I'm downstairs with my mom & dad   they want to go to the store   I have to

Stay here   I don't want to   I sit & cry   grandma comes downstairs to watch me

I don't want her to watch me   she smells funny   I cry harder   take me with you

They yell at me   I cry harder   dad gives me a dollar   tells me to stay here

I cry   they leave   I sit on the steps crying   I wanted to go   grandma falls asleep on

The couch   I sit on the steps & wait for mom & dad to come & get me they're

Not here yet   I think they've left me forever & ever   I cry harder   I rip up the dollar

In ten hundred pieces & throw it to the ground   I get scared   maybe dad will be mad

At me   I run upstairs & find grandma's purse   I look for a dollar   a bunch of them are

Hidden in a smelly white bag   I take a dollar & run downstairs   I fall asleep   mom

Wakes me up   dad wants to take me to the store so I can spend my dollar

I can't find it   she helps me look for it   she finds it in my shoe   she laughs   you're

A magic man—she says—you turned a dollar into ten dollars   how'd you do that

My first brush with crime

O' Osiris   are you wrestling with your own demons   come here my liege   give

Them to me   I want to see what haunts a savior

Light explodes in my eyes   I scream   my head feels like it's been sliced open with a

Razor blade

I can see it   a storm brews on the horizon   it plays a trick on Horus

What are you doing   the clouds grow dark & gray   a bolt of lightening assumes the

Dimensions of a man   he stands before you   don't do that   the blood oh god the blood

He tears you to shreds & scatters your remains across the land

O' Osiris I feel it I know what you're going through O' you the pain my joints burn I'm stretched across a nation stop it

Get me out of here I no longer what to share your vision

Mom takes me to a big brick store a bunch of kids are going inside she tells me to

Get out I stand outside & wait for her she tells me that she can't go I climb back

In & tell her that she has to go she laughs & says she can't I cry don't leave me

Mommy

She laughs I don't wanna go I have to she takes me inside I'm surrounded by a bunch of weird looking kids mommy leaves I cry harder this burnt kid with frizzy

Hair laughs at me says I'm mommy's boy I cry harder

Flashes of time streaks of gray & white

Osiris embodiment of holiness O' king of eternity O' mercy standing beside the divine boat give me the strength to finish this give me the wisdom of truth teach me to channel the divine

O' Osiris dreaming of Isis where do you dwell with whom do you break your bread your daily bread what do you fear with whom do you speak when you are afraid where do you go when your time is up

Osiris send me back I don't want to dwell in these caverns anymore Osiris—my dear sweet liege—why aren't you listening to me

Mom is asleep dad's at work my sisters are at school I think I don't know why I'm home I look around the house I'm curious & I'm trying to discover new things I come across this weird tube of junk it has a picture of a naked guy laying on a naked woman on it I feel strange my head feels funny I crawl into a barrel & look at the picture on the tube my thing down there feels strange I pull down my pants & look at it oh my god it's bigger & its really red I pinch some cream out of the tube its cold against my finger

I rub it all over my thing down there I rub it rub it rub it rub it rub it rub it rub it

I don't see what the big deal is anyway

Flashes of time   streaks of gray & white

School was never much fun anyway   everyone makes fun of my last name   they torture me 'cause of my hair   'cause I'm dirty   'cause my mother doesn't clean out the lint tray on the washer   they pick on any & everything   I hate them all   I no longer want to go

So I quit going   mom & dad fight me constantly   Fuck You   I don't want to go   I keep getting expelled because I never show up   thank god   this goes on for years   I don't feel comfortable in my own skin   the principle suggests that I drop out of day school &

Go to alternative school   sounds good to me   mom & dad are hesitant but hey   if it gets me going everyday

O' Osiris   I dream of you   come to me as I have come to you   Where are you   where

With whom am I speaking my dear sweet liege

I'm fifteen   I'm at Adam's house   we're trading comics   Shooting the shit like we

Always do   he won't give me what I want   I try to finagle him   the phone rings

He answers it   & tosses it to me   it's Jamie   she's crying   grandma's dead—she

Says—my heart drops   I can't speak   my aunt gets on the phone   I mistake her for

My mother

She asks if I need a ride home   I tell her no

Adam & I go back to trading comics   I don't break the news to him

I go home a few minutes later   relatives are hanging on the porch they're

Standing in the yard   I don't know what to do   I walk into the hallway & see my

Mother & father standing there   dad's looking up at the staircase mom is

Crying

My cousins emerge from darkness shrouding the top of the

Stairs they're carrying grandma on a gurney she's covered with a sheet I can't

See her O' grandma where have you gone Where are you going Skip cries his

Eyes out as he carries her he turns his head he can't even look at her I don't cry

I never cried I kept it all inside

The funereal the second time I ever saw my father cry the first time I saw him

Cry was when my younger sister had been diagnosed with epilepsy she had a petite

Seizure & dropped her plate it shattered her food was no more she ran out

Of the room crying Dad lost it there was nothing he could do for her

Flashes of time streaks of gray & white

We're in Missouri they're about to bury grandma the ground is hard the

Men are digging graves by hand why are all funerals held on rainy days

All of my relatives are down here everyone raced against time to be here

I stand in the rain & stare down at a tombstone with my name etched on it

Fear rings mutely through my hollow bones they open grandma's coffin seconds

Before they lower her so my cousin Davey can kiss her she has what

Appears to be a smile on her face her skin is pale & green Peggy is

Standing behind me she's clutching her gut crying

Dreams of green flesh

O' Osiris this is when madness kicks in everything that you've been showing

Me has been soaked in innocence this is where I lose it

I soon drop out of school altogether   I soon start smoking pot   I soon start

Stealing   everything means nothing anymore   I am terrified of death   I

Saw my fucking name on a tombstone   nothing means anything these days

I start dating Angie   stole her from Nick   we sleep together   she's my first

Kiss   Jamie   Angie   Mansfield   & I are sitting in my room watching True

Romance   Angie & Jamie are talking about something   they look at me &

Giggle   Mansfield whispers in my ear   tells me that Angie is going to

Sit beside me   when she says hey I gotta tell you something she's gonna kiss

You   my heart beats   O' Osiris I can't take it   I'm terrified

She does what Mansfield says & kisses me   O' Life   nothing means anything

Anymore

Total depraved decadent madness   phantasmagoria   schizophrenic gunshots

Drugs   alcohol   death   poetry   sex   masturbation   fights   running afraid

Everything   nothing   death   love   hate   isolation   loneliness   O' Osiris

What have you done to me

I discover Jim Morrison & The Doors   he introduces me to words through him

I discover Kerouac   Ginsberg   Burroughs   Blake   Whitman   Rimbaud   Joyce

Sophocles   Nietzsche   everything that is holy

I isolate myself & set out to create an identity for myself   I will capture the

Hearts of women & peers through words   I redefine myself & realign my

Senses

I write & write   spitting out well over a million words before my twenty-first

Birthday

Then I meet Linda   she inspires me to be a better person   I try to win her over

With poetry instead of actions   she appears to bite the bait   we go out all the

Time   we kiss   we lay in bed   her juices stain my forearm   she tastes parts of

Me that I never thought would be eaten   the moonlit room scars my eyes   it is

Magical & chaotic   I want her   I need her   I never hear from her again

It crushes me   I realize that a word is only a shell of a thought   nothing

Prepares me for this epiphany   my world is torn in two   I lose faith in poetry

The one thing that gave me hope for six years   then it is gone   gone

& I have nothing to show for it except a scarred mind   I gave up on it for

Two years   then rediscovered it when I realized that only *I* could change

Me

O' Osiris   thank you   thank you for sharing this vision   thank you for showing

Me the way   thank you Osiris   thank you   Osiris   are you listening to me

Osiris   where have you gone

Funny I have a strange feeling I've been alone all along

The Chapter of Understanding

Empty is my heart. Closed is my skull. Hollow are my eyes. Trembling are these   Bones rattling in defiance of the void.

My stomach writhes in blue-lit agony. All forms of silence are redefined in

Its wake.

I am no one. I am everyone. I am the blue hue hiding behind the clouds. I am

The unfettered sun breaking a sweat. I am the shape in the clouds. I am the

Manifestation of the world united. I am nothing. I am everything.

I don't know anymore.

I shall come to an end before I've developed. I shall never come to an

End. Never shall I come to an end.

Texts relating to the Conferences of the holy Trinity

The Madman: "O' Osiris—wake from your tomb, step out of your temple &

Bring me kicking & screaming into this world. For I have lingered in the

Meats of your shadow

Far too long.

I glimpse the world through false eyes and

slip back into the void.

O' Holy one! I like what I've seen! I want to see, feel, taste, speak, hear,

& Foresee it all!
Wave your crooked scepter & set me free!"

Osiris: "O' Madman—to whom do you speak? For I am useless now,
Having been spread throughout this land against my will.
I desire to be whole again so I can grant your every wish
& cure you of this
Despair.
Alas I am but a shell of what I once was. For death met me at an
Early age & I am married to this tomb.
To help you I must first seek out Ka
& ask for his forgiveness."

Ka: "Don't look at me. You two are on your own."

Arc of the Seven Arits

The First Arit

The name of the Angel is Aaron. The name of the Angel is Nick. The name of The angel is Tracy.

When the Madman arrives he will dust off these Angels & place them upon his Restored hearth, saying: "To those who helped form my consciousness. Tho' I See you not you are still in my thoughts. Blessed be he who helped raise me. Blessed be he!" & they are forever hung on the walls of his temple (youth).

The Second Arit

The name of the Angel is Mansfield. The name of the Angel is Jit. The name of The Angel is Adam.

When the Madman arrives he will say unto thee: "Why have you forsaken Me? I am still He who thinks of you. Do not allow my memory to sully the Present. Blessed be he who helped form me. Blessed be he!" & they are Forever hung on the walls of his temple (life).

The Third Arit

The name of the Angel is Tim. The name of the Angel is James. The name of The Angel is Bildhauser.

When the Madman arrives he will say unto thee: "Things will change & all will be well. For once I trusted you & I am wiser for having done So. I learned from you. Now I give to you. Blessed be he who helps form me. Blessed be he!" & they are forever hung on the walls of his temple (life).

The Fourth Arit

The name of the Angel is Angie. The name of the Angel is Lindsey. The name of The Angel is Sandy.

When the Madman arrives he will lay these Angels down & say: "O' You! Homage to thee! Where once you were forgotten you would now be Replaced! 'Tis the passions of youth that remain! Blessed be she who helped Spoil me! Blessed be she!" & they are forever discarded in the halls of his Temple (repression).

The Fifth Arit

The name of the Angel is Emily. The name of the Angel is Dawn. The name of The Angel is Linda.

When the Madman arrives he will dust off these Angels & give them a just Funeral, saying: "O' Angels! Those who once tortured me! I give you to the Ages & set a piece of myself on the pyre! Blessed be she who helped curse Me. Blessed be She!" & they are forever buried in the mausoleum in his Temple (death).

The Sixth Arit

The name of the Angel is Peggy. The name of the Angel is Jamie. The name of The Angel is Cody. The name of the Angel is Ashley. The name of the Angel is Kaitlynn.

When the Madman arrives he will say unto thee: "O' Angels! Homage To thee! I give you this wine, this blessed wine, in thanks for helping form me! Blessed be those who continue to inspire me! Blessed be they!" & they are Forever allowed into the sacred halls of my temple (life).

The Seventh Arit

The name of the Angel is Leon. The name of the Angel is Shelia. The name of The Angel is Callie.

When the Madman arrives he will say unto thee: "Thank you, heavens, for giving Me life, for teaching me all things are holy! Thank you for allowing me to grow in my own garden! Thank you O' Life, I love you! Blessed be those who gave me life. Blessed be they!" & they stood strong when they constructed His fragile Temple (life).

The Chapter of giving oneself

To his heart

The scribe of the Osiris of Ani—future madman & anarchist—

Saith:

"I have stood by long enough & watched as temples

Collapse around me. I have felt the psychic tremors. I
Have
Envisioned new worlds but I've never explored them.
I have carried aborted Angels even tho' they broke their
Wings on
Purpose.
I have smelled the rotting flesh on my own arm. I have
Written too many books from the
Grave.
Now I give myself to thee in order to rebuild my temple.
From there I will board this divine
Boat
&
Float up the forgotten river."

The Chapter of Not
Giving up

O' thou who art depressed, O' thou who art depressed, O' thou
Whose depression glows in the gloom of winter, O' thou
Who
Tastes the divine absurdity,
O' thou whose looking glass is spoiled with tarnished
Reflections
O' thou whose depression has developed a taste for his
Own flesh
O' thou who carves pock marks into his empty soul
O' thou
Who art frightened because he no longer cares
What tomorrow

Brings
O' thou who art depressed, O' thou who art depressed, O' thou
Whose depression glows in the gloom of winter, give thyself
Unto thee.
Thy shall not be depressed, thy shall not be decayed—thy shall
Never decay—thy shall not collapse, thy shall not die by
Thine own hands
As long as thy puts blind faith into my rapidly
Developing
Plan.

Chapter relating to the
Heresy of Oneself

Homage to thee, O' Loves of my life, who beat back my brow with
Their crooked smiles
Homage to thee, O' Heart of my loins, who taketh the air from my
Lungs
Homage to thee, O' Villainous despair, whose blue hues continue to
Haunt me
Homage to thee, O' Great depression, who continues to haunt me &
To inspire me even though I try to ignore you
Homage to thee, O' Words, it is you that has gotten me into this
mess, I
Don't resent you
Homage to thee, O' Dear sweet friends, who grow distant by the
ever
Expanding hour
Homage to thee, O' Mother, who gave me this unwavering fetish for
Big, succulent eyes

Homage to thee, O' Father, who gave me everything save a sense of
Coherent timing

Homage to thee, O' Osiris, whose peaceful eye illuminates the
Heavens

Homage to thee, O' Muse, who resurrected the silent Osiris in a flash
Of confused inspiration

Homage to thee, O' Heart, who continues to get me into these
Unfavorable messes

Homage to thee, O' Ka, whom I fear is doomed to lick the boot
Heels of eternity

Hymn to Ka
in Praise of Recognition

O' Madman! Scribe of the Osiris of Ani! Scribe of this chapter!
Where have you
Been rotting? Where were you when you developed these notions?
Where are
You now?
What sphinx has crossed your eyes? What kingdom
Would abolish such a frightened angel?
Who
Here
Protests the restoration of your perilous temple?
Who here dreams of elation? I know who you are
Dear sweet Madman
I've chased you through the centuries
Cool hand scars the back of my cheek
But wait
It is Ka—the unified psyche

Ka the lover of doom
Ka the prophet of chaos
Ka the mistress of intercourse
Ka the moist cunt in the palm of my hand
It is Ka that creams the cock & tastes the salt
Ka that sleeps out of boredom
Ka that dreams of elation
Ka that kicks down the doors
Ka that sways to the slave master
Ka *is* the slave master
It is Ka that cries in the moonlight
Ka that fears the sunrise
Ka that drowns in sorrow
Ka that chokes on aborted Epiphanies
Ka that laments his past
Ka that denounces Christ
Ka that longs for Christ
Ka that renounces everything that has ever come before him
Ka that admires everything that has come before him
It is Ka that represents ego
Ka that swallows the symbolist's flesh
Ka that drowns in his essence
Ka that misses his grandmother
Ka that fears death
Ka that can't get to sleep
Ka that fucks mute phantoms
Ka that mutes fucked phantoms
Ka that fears the world
Ka that accepts the world
Ka that writes in his secret journals

Ka that publishes his works on his skin
Ka that expresses the ineffable
Ka that ignores the omnipresent
Ka that is everything that's wrong
It is Ka that sleeps on my pillow
Ka that wakes in my head
Ka that dreams of tomorrow
Ka that soaks in the light
Ka that resents his parents
Ka that falls in love with strangers
Ka that can't quench his thirst
Ka that struggles to find life
Ka that's tortured since birth
Ka that shares my tired forgotten name
O' Madman! Scribe of the Osiris of Ani! Scribe of this chapter!
    Where have you
Been rotting?

About the Author

Julius Henry was born into a family of sideshow freaks. His mother was the bearded lady and his father was lobster-boy. He is in no way different or unique, which, he supposes, makes him the freak in his freak family. He can be reached at julius_hnry@yahoo.com.

www.ingramcontent.com/pod-product-compliance
Lightning Source LLC
LaVergne TN
LVHW011418080426
835512LV00005B/121